AFTER THE TROJAN WAR

Three Plays
WOMEN OF TROY
HECUBA
HELEN

AFTER THE TROJAN WAR

WOMEN OF TROY
HECUBA
HELEN

Three plays by
Euripides

translated and introduced by
Kenneth McLeish

a b s o l u t e   c l a s s i c s

INTRODUCTION

Euripides

Euripides was born in 485BCE or 480BCE, and died in 406BCE.
His first production was in 455BCE, and he wrote some 92 plays
altogether. With Aeschylus and Sophocles he forms the grand trio of
Athenian tragic dramatists: all extant 'Greek tragedies' are their
work. Nineteen of Euripides' plays survive, a dozen more than from
either Aeschylus or Sophocles. The titles of his other plays are
known, and show that he favoured stories with women protagonists
- and since Greek playwrights usually acted in their own plays, this
in turn suggests that he may have been skilled in the art of travesty
acting, which was as highly regarded in Athenian theatre as in the
Japanese Noh and Kabuki traditions of later years.

With few exceptions, Athenian tragedians based their plays on stories from myth. These stories often involved the interaction of
human beings with supernatural powers and forces, and were linked
to the historical legends and social rituals of particular communities.
(The Orestes myth, for example, was localised in Argos.) The
myths would have been as familiar to the audience as stories of King
Arthur or Noah might be to a British audience today. The dramatist
concentrated on specific incidents from his chosen myth, presenting
and shaping them both to draw out their latent drama and also to
make general points about human character, the interaction of
humans and humans or of humans and the supernatural. The plays
were originally performed at huge competitive festivals, and prizes
seem to have been awarded less for novelty than for the poetic and
musical quality of the play, and for the particular spin each author
put on familiar themes and well-worn material.

The surviving plays suggest that Euripides may have been an entirely different kind of dramatist from either Aeschylus or Sophocles.
Aeschylus' surviving plays are sonorous poetic explorations of such
grand themes as destiny, freewill, inherited guilt and obligation.
Sophocles' surviving work is formally elegant (though its stylistic
limpidity often contrasts with the racked emotions and ironical
deceptions which he depicts), and he is especially interested in the
way human beings respond to their perception of the workings of
fate and the supernatural - forces which he, the dramatist, never

seems to question. Euripides, in the surviving plays, took a different line from either. His language is neither as sublime as Aeschylus' nor as evenly-paced as Sophocles'; indeed it is often abrupt, slangy and matter-of-fact to the point of bathos. All three plays in the present volume, for example, at their most intense moments, happily incorporate puns, jokes and extraordinarily formal, almost self-mocking rhetoric. He takes a sardonic, utilitarian approach to the basic stories, changing them, exploring odd corners in unusual ways, treating their weirder events with deadpan reverence as if they were gospel truth - and he often veers from one approach to another in the same scene, even the same speech or line. In all his surviving plays, language serves hectic dramatic articulation, a torrent of ideas, argument, and visual and conceptual *coups de théâtre* as startling (especially to people brought up on the notion that Greek tragedy is stuffy and boring) as they are spectacular.

Euripides is outstanding at showing characters in states of emotional and psychological stress, and manipulates each situation, each myth, to do so. His plays are written with consistent irony, so that we always seem to be being told more than is superficially there; in the Trojan War plays this is given a dark, bleak edge whose nearest modern counterpart is in the work of Dürrenmatt or Albee. 'Euripidean irony' also involves writing about terrible events and powerful dilemmas in simple, even clichéd language, so that there is a continuous 'pull' between what is being shown and the way he shows it. (In passing, this aspect of his art has often been neglected by translators into English, even such fine craftsmen as William Arrowsmith or Philip Vellacott. They have gone all out for 'literary' English, making high-flown and flowery what is actually extremely plain, even bathetic; it is as if they were reluctant to allow the flickering moods and swoops of literary 'level' to make their own effect. In a manner not paralleled in English-language theatre until our present century, Euripides left his actors a great deal of creative space. He allowed them, so to speak, to fill in the thought between the words - and translations should follow, not reverse, this trend.)

The unpredictable theatricality in Euripides' work, coupled with irreverence towards both the gods and the politics of Periclean Athens, gained him a reputation for wildness. Although his plays were always news - he is referred to, and commented on, more than any other ancient dramatist - they seldom won high prizes at the religious festivals where they were first performed. At the peak of his

career, he was prosecuted (unsuccessfully) for impiety, and in his
eighties, during the anti-intellectual purges which led, later, to the
trial and execution of Socrates, he was forced to escape from Athens
to Macedonia, controversial and unregenerate to the last.

Euripides and the Trojan War

The Trojan War cycle is one of the most substantial in all Greek
myth. Since every Greek state was held to have sent men to fight in
the War, its events were part of the founding myths of most cities,
and the details of the War itself blend supernatural and human
action in a way, and to an extent, paralleled by no other surviving
cycle. Gods and humans collaborated to build the city; the War
started because humans rashly became involved in a quarrel among
the gods; during the conflict gods, like humans, ranged themselves
on either side, so that the end of the War required a sorting out in
Heaven, a revision of attitudes, just as drastic as it did on Earth.

All this seems to have fascinated Euripides. Something like one third
of his entire output uses themes from the Trojan myth-cycle, and
half a dozen of his extant plays develop particular stories in detail.
He usually deals not with the War itself, but with its aftermath, and
makes powerful points about the futility of fighting, the nature of
patriotism, honour and glory, the duty owed by conquerors to con-
quered, the collapse of moral and ethical correlatives in human life -
and, most especially, about the position of women, caught up in the
fighting but even more deeply involved in its effects.

In his lifetime, Euripides was mocked as a misogynist. (This may
have been because he put so many of his women characters through
such torment - it ranges from the pangs of 'impossible' love to madness, from desertion to rape, from child-murder to slavery.) In fact,
few dramatists of any period have written more extensively, or better, about women. All his plays contain bravura female parts, and
several of them (Medea, Phaedra, Iphigenia, Hecuba) are among the
finest roles in western literature. The Choruses in many plays,
including all three in this volume, are women, and articulate femi-
nine viewpoints as well as merely punctuating or commenting on the
action (as Greek Choruses are traditionally, and wrongly, supposed
to have done). Writing for male actors and a male audience,
Euripides explores women's psychology at all levels. Of the plays in
this book, *Women of Troy* and *Hecuba* are concerned with the preoc-
cupations, tensions and attitudes which women of Euripides' time

might have had to war and to 'men's games'; the central theme of *Helen* is the balance between the reputed character of Helen (that is as the incarnation of amoral, seductive beauty) and her 'real' nature - and how this balance affects not only her herself, but everyone involved with her. We can only speculate about how such roles may have been performed (by men in travesty) in the ancient theatre. But modern actors find a depth, range and truth in Euripides' writing for women which is unrivalled till the work of Shakespeare or Ibsen, and which yields little in quality to either of those dramatists.

Women of Troy, *Hecuba* and *Helen* are not connected: Euripides did not write trilogies, in the manner of (say) Aeschylus' *Oresteia*. Each play shows the aftermath of the Trojan War from a separate viewpoint, and draws out different aspects of the myth. *Women of Troy* is set among a group of captives waiting to be shipped from Troy as slaves, the day after the city's destruction. Queen Hecuba comforts them, and leads them in mourning for their loved ones and for their city and country ravaged. She is a tower of strength to them, and we see what this steadfastness costs her. The Greeks take Cassandra, her daughter, and Astyanax, her grandson, and she is forced to bear it. The play is a magnificent display of mourning, a devastating account of the misery and waste of war. *Hecuba* has a similar setting, the day after the fall of Troy. But this time Hecuba is shown as someone driven to the edge of insanity by suffering. Her hopes reside in the survival of her last two children. First she is forced to beg for the life of her daughter Polyxena - to no avail. Then she finds that her son Polydorus has been treacherously killed. These events tip her over the brink of sanity, first into hysterical grief and then into a revenge as horrible as Medea's, as implacable as Lady Macbeth's plotting. The part is bravura and the effect magnificent. *Helen* takes place seven years after the end of the War. In Egypt - treated as a backwater, far from 'real' events - Helen waits anxiously for her husband Menelaus to rescue her. She knows nothing about the War, since she was taken away by the gods before it started; the 'Helen' for whom Greeks and Trojans fought was a shadow, so that the entire Trojan enterprise was doubly futile. The contrast between Helen's true character and her reputation is only the first of many surprises as Menelaus at last arrives and the play proceeds.

Original staging

Euripides' plays were first produced in the Theatre of Dionysus,
outside the god's shrine at the foot of the Acropolis in Athens. Each
was part of a competitive religious and dramatic festival, before an
audience of some 14,000 people. Each playwright directed his plays
(three or four, on a single day), arranged the choreography, played
the leading roles, and perhaps also composed the music. There were
three actors, all male. In *Women of Troy* the first actor played
Hecuba, the second Athene, Cassandra, Andromache and Helen,
and the third Poseidon, Talthybius and Menelaus. In *Hecuba* the
first actor played Hecuba; there is no certainty about which parts the
other actors played, though the musical demands on Polyxena and
Polymestor suggest that they may have been taken by the same per-
former. In *Helen* the first actor played Helen (and possibly the
Servant and/or Castor), the second Menelaus (and possibly Teucer
and/or Castor), the third all the other parts, notably the three
'Egyptians' (Doorkeeper, Theonoe, Theoclymenus). A Chorus of
15, all male, sang and danced; their leader also took part in the spoken dialogue. There were (silent) attendants, and a number of musi-
cians, probably playing flute, lyre, drum and cymbal or tambourine.

Something like half of each play was declaimed or sung with instru-
mental accompaniment and formal movement. Rhythmic organisa-
tion was quantitative (not by stress, as in English verse), and the
lines fell into patterns of long and short syllables which also deter-
mined the rhythm of the music and the dance-steps. In the choruses, there were sections of *strophe* and *antistrophe*, the rhythm of one
section repeating that of the lines before, and the themes balancing
and contrasting in a similar way. The dialogue, especially in *Hecuba*,
is often patterned by rhetorical correspondence, in which each point
made for one side is countered, later, by a point for the other, as in
modern law-court oratory. Different metrical patterns, by conven-
tion, had different emotional associations. The music was in single
overlapping lines without harmony, in the manner we now associate
with Arabian or Far Eastern music. The verse moves between
speech (usually in iambics, analogous to English blank verse) and
declamation or song (usually in lyric metres). Some scenes are
exclusively speech or lyric; others intersperse the two modes.

A feature of the plays, as of all Greek tragedy, is a number of short
ejaculations: *oee, moee, otototot oee, feoo, E!* (short, like the 'e' in 'hen')
and so on. Each is used in specific circumstances, and seems to have

had specific meaning. They were probably not onomatopoeic, but were instructions to the actors to improvise particular kinds of vocal or musical melismas. They are not intended to be performed exactly as written. (In workshops, actors have found that in many cases inhaled or exhaled breaths work well.) Their exact meanings are now lost. The various permutations of *o*, *mo* and *ee* were cries of grief or pain. *Feoo* seems to have been a sound of surprise, approval or disapproval, used where modern Greeks might say '*Po-po-po-po*' or English people might tut their tongues. In most translations these ejaculations are omitted, or replaced with such English anodynes as 'Alas!' or 'Woe!'; in this book I have simply transliterated, leaving the actors to interpret. At one point in *Hecuba*, Polymestor breaks into a kind of savage war-cry, summoning help: this was probably a large musical effect, analogous to the dressing of Astyanax for burial in *Women of Troy*. I have left parts of it in Greek.

Women of Troy

Women of Troy was first performed (with three other, unconnected plays, now lost) in 415BCE, and won second prize. Two years before, the islanders of Melos had refused to support Athens against Sparta in the Peloponnesian War, and the Athenians had retaliated by sacking the island, slaughtering its men and boys and enslaving its women. The morality of this act was hotly debated at the time - and two years later, before an Athenian audience many of whom may have taken part in what happened, and who may have had Melian women at home as slaves, Euripides chose to present, in *Women of Troy*, a pointed depiction of the effects of such a siege, in a clear (if largely unstated) context of disapproval. Not only that, but before an audience which was largely or exclusively male, he put his arguments in the mouths of women - at a time when women in Athens seldom took part in public life, and when there was even serious discussion (at least among males) about whether females possessed any intelligence or moral understanding whatsoever.

These factors, coupled with the play's enormous theatrical energy, must have given it an edge of danger quite unsettling to the audience - and Euripides compounded this, at a religious festival, by giving his leading character several uncompromising assertions that the gods (if they exist at all) are deaf or callous to human needs.

In the days when classical scholars derived their ideas about Greek tragedy not from the plays but from Aristotle's treatise *Poetics*,

Women of Troy was regularly criticised because 'nothing happened'
in it. This is true only in the limited sense that it has no ongoing
narrative plot, no *coups-de-théâtre*, no exposition of how the 'tragic
flaw' of some character leads him or her to challenge the gods and to
be punished for it. In performance, the play's dramatic articulation
is compelling. It explores not a consequential sequence of events but
a single situation and the characters in that situation. Hecuba and
her companions - and, in a different way, the Greeks - are trapped.
All past certainties are swept away; morals and ethics must be
remembered or reinvented. Those characters who rely on the past -
notably Cassandra and Andromache - are remorselessly stripped of
all they have; the women of the Chorus ignorantly, innocently, speculate about a future which is as unpredictable and exciting as a
dream; as the play progresses we see Hecuba gradually drawing
strength from the only source available to her, the very hopelessness
of her situation, putting the past ceremoniously behind her and
learning how to face, and control, her own and others' future.

The only other surviving play as 'static' as this one is Aeschylus'
Seven Against Thebes - and dons have attacked that, too, on the
grounds that because it fails to fit Aristotle's categories it is not 'true
tragedy'. In fact the categories are wrong in so many respects - particularly with regard to both Aeschylus and Euripides - that this is
no argument at all. Even if it were, the chances are high that both
Seven Against Thebes and *Women of Troy* conform to a different kind
of play altogether, one which has not survived and was not discussed
by Aristotle, in which stasis (absence of developmental action)
rather than drama (performed action) is the nature of the experience. To say that the play lacks 'drama' is as ridiculous as would be
finding the same fault in (say) Bach's *St Matthew Passion*. *Women of
Troy* may be formally different from most surviving Greek tragedies,
but it is also one of the masterpieces of the genre.

Hecuba

Hecuba was first performed in about 424BCE, some ten years
before *Women of Troy*. Its companion-plays are not known; neither is
the prize it won. It comes at the mid-point of Euripides' career, in
his most prolific period. Like *Women of Troy*, it has nothing in common with the kind of Greek tragedy described by Aristotle. It
belongs to another group ignored by him: plays which explore the
character of an individual driven to extreme behaviour by great suffering. Sophocles' *Electra* and Aeschylus' *Prometheus Bound* are plays

of this type, as are Euripides' own *Medea* and *Heracles*. Though *Hecuba* shares with *Women of Troy* a concern about the effects of war and women's condition in general, it narrows the focus, making the men ciphers and concentrating on Hecuba's own state of mind, on her journey from despair to fury, and on the events which trigger it.

The style of *Hecuba* is remarkably rhetorical. Its manner is almost as self-conscious as that of (say) Racine's *Britannicus*, and there is a large amount of music and distracted song. (Hecuba's first 'speech', and Polymestor's outbursts after he is blinded and after the final debate, are typical: in the original staging, they may have been performed in a manner we nowadays associate less with tragedy than with Far Eastern theatre or even opera.) Throughout the play, dislocation between dramatic style and the almost melodramatic intensity of the emotions gives a kind of over-riding irony, far subtler and more unsettling than the overt irony of (say) Hecuba's first confrontation with Polymestor or the constant stressing of Agamemnon's temporising and vanity. Such technical dislocation (which can hardly be accidental) may strike chords with theatregoers today. But it has damned the play's reputation with scholars. Dons down the ages have complained that *Hecuba* is broken-backed, that it is artistically incompetent to write a first half in which your central character is all grief and a second half in which she is all rage. This may appear to be the case in the study, but in the theatre – as in real life – it can seem an entirely plausible way for someone of this character, in these circumstances, to behave. Apparent oddity, in fact, both mirrors human experience and 'makes' the play.

Helen
Helen was first performed in 412BCE, two or three years after *Women of Troy* – and, incidentally, one year before Aristophanes' *Thesmophoriazusai (Festival Time)*, which parodies it mercilessly. It was performed on the same occasion as, though not in tandem with, another surviving play, *Andromeda* – and like that belongs to yet another type of Euripidean tragedy ignored by Aristotle, the one scholars nowadays call 'romances'. In these plays (others, from the same period, are *Iphigenia in Tauris* and *Ion*) action is propelled by a light, fast-moving plot full of surprises, coincidences and implausibilities, and the endings are less tragic than like fairy-tale, with the gods intervening to ensure that the leading characters live happily ever afterwards. There are opportunities for spectacular music and dance – sometimes not closely related to the main plot – and the dia-

logue is written not in strictly-corseted tragic metres but in a conversational style like that of Euripides' friend and contemporary Aristophanes, and disparagingly called (by him) *lalia*, 'chit-chat'.

Characteristically, Euripides uses this light-hearted form and style for deeper purposes than it might suggest. The central idea of *Helen* – the only part of the story he did not himself invent – is that the Helen who went to Troy was a phantom, a cloud-puppet made by Hera, and the real Helen spent the war-years languishing in Egypt. The Helen we see is thus an ordinary, decent, long-suffering wife who just happens to be the most beautiful woman in the world and to be plagued by the reputation unjustly heaped on her as a result of the antics of her double. Euripides explores the duality between appearance and reality not only in the character of Helen herself, but throughout the action. Is Menelaus the boastful windbag his appearances in other plays (*Women of Troy*, for example) might lead us to expect, or the long-suffering, Odysseus-like traveller he now claims to be? Is Theonoe a servant of truth and honour, or a schemer against her own brother? Most striking of all – a consistent theme in all the 'romances' – are the gods honest and concerned for human morality and happiness, or devious, malevolent frauds playing with mortal destinies as children play with toys?

Again in common with many of the later romances, *Helen* also deals with another un-Aristotelian theme: human love – in this case, between long-separated, middle-aged people. Only one other surviving Euripides play, *Alcestis*, so movingly shows the affection between people long-married, offering us real characters rather than the lay-figure husbands and wives of such plays as (say) *King Oedipus* or *Agamemnon*. His concentration on the humanity of his characters, and the dislocation between the truth-to-life of their emotions and the bizarre events of the plots he places them in, may remind modern readers and spectators of late Shakespeare: *Pericles* and *A Winter's Tale* are close in mood to *Helen*, and that mood is one not of tragedy or even 'romance' but of transcendental fairy-tale, the supernatural entering human lives not to blight them or give them stern direction, but to irradiate them with calm after storm, with the happiness of suffering survived.

Kenneth McLeish, 1995

WOMEN OF TROY

The première production of this translation was given by Classics on a Shoestring at the Gate Theatre, London, on July 16th 1991. Paola Dionissotti played HECUBA, Barbara Flynn ANDROMACHE, Kathryn Hunter CASSANDRA, Kristin Hewson HELEN, James Purefoy TALTHYBIUS, Paul Brennan MENELAUS and POSEIDON, Cheryl Moskowitz ATHENE, and the WOMEN OF TROY were Nicola Burnett Smith, Siobhan Fogarty, Cate Hamer, Emma Rice, Susannah Rickards, Sadie Shimmin and Zara Turner. The play was directed by Katie Mitchell, the desighner was Peter Ruthven Hall, music direction was by Ben Livingstone and lighting design was by Mark Agar and David Ludlum.

The first production on the Olivier Stage of the Royal National Theatre was on March 16th 1995. Rosemary Harris played HECUBA, Jane Birkin ANDROMACHE, Josette Bushell-Mingo CASSANDRA, Janie Dee HELEN, Philip Whitchurch TALTHYBIUS, Peter McEnery MENELAUS, Leo Wringer POSEIDON and Robert Pickavance ATHENE. The WOMEN OF TROY were played by Selma Alispahic, Jacqueline Dankworth, Soussana Farroknia, Jenny Howe, Shelley King, Carol Leader, Elizabeth Mansfield, Leonie Mellinger, Soudabeh Neeya, Toshie Ogura, Gabrielle Reidy and Jax Williams. Will Barton, Dimeon Defoe and Clive Wedderburn played Greek soldiers. The play was directed by Annie Castledine, the associate director was Annabel Arden, the designer was Iona McLeish, music direction was by Adrian Johnston and lighting design was by Nick Beadle.

CHARACTERS

POSEIDON
ATHENE
HECUBA
TALTHYBIUS
CASSANDRA
ANDROMACHE
MENELAUS
HELEN

ATTENDANTS, SOLDIERS, THE CHILD ASTYANAX [silent parts]

CHORUS OF TROJAN WOMEN

No man's land, between the shattered walls of Troy and the tents of the victorious Greeks. Night. Enter Poseidon.

POSEIDON: You see Poseidon. From my palace,
       Where nymphs tread graceful dances
       Deep in salty sea, I come here to Troy.
       Long years ago, on this Trojan plain,
       Two gods, Apollo and Poseidon - I -
       Laid stone on stone,
       Raised high these towers,
       True to the line. My heart was here.
       My city. Burned, torn down, destroyed.
       Greek spearsmen sacked it.
       By Athene's plan
       Epeus of Phocis built a wooden horse -
       Pegged timbers, pregnant with soldiers -
       Saw it dragged inside. Full-bellied,
       Big with spears -
       A common tale, a famous tale,
       In years to come. No people now.
       Empty shrines. God's holy ground
       Paddled with blood. Lord Zeus' shrine,
       Zeus Protector, fouled.
       They butchered Priam there,
       Made altar steps their killing-ground.
       They stripped the gold, the loot of Troy,
       Stacked it for shipping home. Fair wind:
       That's all they wait for now,
       Fair wind home, to wives, children,
       The welcome they've dreamt of now
       For ten long years. I too must go,
       Outmatched by goddesses -
       Hera, Athene, who favoured Greece,
       Who toppled Troy - must leave
       These cloud-capp'd towers, these altars:
       In a city of ghosts,
       Who crooks the knee to gods?

How they wail,
The women, prisoners of war,
Thin voices along Scamander's banks,
As they wait to be... distributed.
Some know their future homes already:
Arcadia, Thessaly, Athens.
Others wait, here in these tents. Unallocated still.
Spoils for Their Lordships,
The kings of Greece.
Helen's there, Tyndareus' daughter,
Queen of Sparta,
In the chains she so rightly earned.
Here - see, beside the gate -
Unhappy Hecuba, all tears.
How she must weep! Her city,
Her people, gone. Have they told her yet
How Polyxena, her daughter, died,
Blood-sacrifice at Achilles' tomb?
Her husband Priam, their children,
Slipped away.
Cassandra, the mad one,
The virgin, Apollo's dregs:
Now Agamemnon's spoil,
Spoiled in his bed
In the teeth of justice,
Of respect for God.
Troy, farewell. How proud you were -
Your towers, your walls!
How strong you stood
Till Athene, Zeus' daughter,
Smashed you down.

Enter Athene.

ATHENE: May it please you, Majesty,
                 Brother of Zeus my father,
                 May I lay old enmity aside, and speak?

POSEIDON: Athene, queen of heaven! Close kin -
     All enmity's charmed away. Speak on.

ATHENE: Your majesty is gracious. Lord,
     What I say concerns us both.

POSEIDON: New word from heaven? From Zeus?
     Some other god... ?

ATHENE: I ask your help, your power. For Troy,
     This ground we walk on. Help me, lord.

POSEIDON: You hated Troy before. Have you come
     To weep, now, when it's burnt to ash?

ATHENE: Will you hear me, lord,
     Hear me and help?

POSEIDON: First, answer: have you come
     To help Greeks or Trojans?

ATHENE: My former enemies, the Trojans:
     I'll gladden them, and prick the Greeks.

POSEIDON: You prance from mind to mind...
     You hate, you love. What reason - ?

ATHENE: My shrine was trampled too.

POSEIDON: When Ajax snatched Cassandra.

ATHENE: And no Greek punished him.

POSEIDON: Though your cunning gave them Troy.

ATHENE: Will you help me to hurt them now?

POSEIDON:	What do you want for them?
ATHENE:	Sour homecoming. Bitter joy.

POSEIDON: On land, or on salty sea?

ATHENE: As they sail away from Troy.
Lord Zeus will send rainstorms,
Hailstones like boulders, hurricanes.
He'll lend me thunderbolts
To hurl at them, to char their ships.
Your part:
Flay all the sea to foam, pile waves,
Stir whirlpools, choke every bay
With drowned Greek flesh.
They'll learn – they must learn –
To accept my yoke, to smile as they bow,
To me and all other gods.

POSEIDON: Ask no more. Your prayer is granted.
I'll stir the sea. I'll glut the shores
With corpse-flesh: beaches of Mykonos,
Headlands of Caphereus,
Reefs of Lemnos, Delos, Skyros.
Climb the sky,
Take Zeus' thunderbolts,
Watch for Greeks, full sail.
When mortals rape cities, temples,
Graves, they condemn themselves.
They destroy; they die.

*Exeunt Poseidon and Athene. Music. Hecuba lifts
herself from where she has been sleeping.*

HECUBA: Up, wretch. Cursed of the gods,
Look up. Troy's gone.
No city now. No queen. All's changed.
God's changed. Endure.
Sail with the current, sail with God.

Life's stormy now. Sail with the current,
Don't butt the waves.
Aee aee, aee aee.
What's left, what's left but tears?
Country, children, husband gone,
Wealth scattered, gone.
Shh!
Why?
Why choke back tears? Why weep?
God presses me down,
Bears down on me,
Racking me, racking me.
Head! Face! Ribs!
Sit up... row...
Comfort in misery,
Comfort in endless tears.

Ships came.
Oars furrowed purple sea.
From Greece, from shelter,
You raced for holy Troy.
Flutes, whistles,
Aee aee, aee aee, you anchored,
Woven cables,
The bay, the lap of Troy,
You tracked her,
Menelaus' wife, no wife,
Helen. They blush, they spit on her,
Her brothers, her country,
Who butchered Priam,
My Priam, left fifty children fatherless,
Ran me aground, Hecuba,
Beached me here in tears.

I crouch by Agamemnon's tent,
A slave,
Dragged from my home,

Shorn grey hair, booty.
O women of Troy,
Our city burns,
Our warriors are gone,
Our daughters raped.
Weep, weep.
As a mother bird
Screams for nestlings lost,
So now I cry.
Once I sang a different song,
Praised gods of Troy,
Led the sacred dance,
While Priam - Priam! -
Leaned on his sceptre, smiled.

Enter some of the Chorus.

CHORUS A: Hecuba, these tears, these cries,   [*strophe*]
              What is it? Something new.
              Inside, in our ruined homes,
              We heard you. Fear tears our hearts.
              What is it?

HECUBA: Children: Greek oarsmen,
              Moving, boarding.

CHORUS A: Oee! What of us, now?
              Will they cargo us, for Greece?

HECUBA: I know what you know.
              A guess: no more.

CHORUS A: Eeoh eeoh.
              Women, gather, come,
              Hear future pain.
              The Greeks set sail.

HECUBA: E! E!
Leave Cassandra.
Poor, mad girl,
Don't bring her.
She'll embarrass them, the Greeks,
Her raving, she'll stab the heart.
Yoh, Troy,
Troy of our hearts,
Troy of our sorrows,
We weep for you.

More women gather.

CHORUS B: Majesty, shivering, afraid,   [*antistrophe*]
We come from the tents,
Greek tents, to hear you. What is it?
Will they kill us now? Will they row,
Beat sea to foam?

HECUBA: Children, since dawn
I've waited, trembled.

CHORUS B: Have orders come?
Oee! Whose slave am I?

HECUBA: Soon enough, you'll know.

Chorus B: Eeoh, eeoh.
Where will they take me?
To Argos? Phthia? An island,
Far away from Troy?

HECUBA: E! E!
Who'll own me now?
Who'll order me?
An old woman, a slave, all tears,
A husk, a ghost, a withered wreath?
Aee aee,

Must I open doors for them,
Nanny their children,
Who once was queen of Troy?

CHORUS: Aee aee, aee aee,   [*strophe*]
                 How will you grieve
                 For the fate that wastes us now?
                 No more shall I twist the shuttle,
                 To and fro, to and fro in Troy.
                 No more see my parent's home,
                 No more. Worse torments wait:
                 Bedmate of Greeks
                 (God snatch it away,
                 That night, that fate!); water-slave,
                 Bent at the spring, carrying, carrying.
                 Pirene's spring! Athens!
                 If only it were so!
                 May I never see eddying Eurotas,
                 Curtsey to Spartan Helen, to Menelaus,
                 City-sacker, who took our Troy.

                 If not to Athens,   [*antistrophe*]
                 Blessed by the gods,
                 Let them take me
                 To the second place I know:
                 Tempe, lovely land, where Peneus flows,
                 Where Olympus deep-rooted stands,
                 Teeming, blossoming –
                 God send me there!
                 Or else where Sicily, Hephaestus' island,
                 Mother of mountains,
                 Stares at Carthage across the sea,
                 Grows posies, garlands of heroes.
                 Or that other land, perhaps,
                 Where Crathis' sweet waters flow,
                 Wet-nurse of warriors, who suckles them,
                 Gives their hair the red glint of gold.

Music ends.

CHORUS: Someone's coming. Some spokesman
               From the Greeks. Falling over himself
               With news. What more can he tell us?
               We know we're slaves.

               Enter Talthybius, attended. [In the original, dur-
               ing the scene which follows, he spoke while Hecuba
               sang, to music.]

TALTHYBIUS: Hecuba... woman... you know me.
               You've seen me before, often,
               Carrying messages
               From the Greek commanders.
               Talthybius, with news.

HECUBA: Women, friends, our fears come true.

TALTHYBIUS: You've been allocated.
               Was that what you feared?

HECUBA: Aee aee!
               Where must they go?
               Thebes? Thessaly?
               Where?

TALTHYBIUS: Each chosen by lot,
               Each by a different man.

HECUBA: Which man? Which woman?
               Is it joy, or tears?

TALTHYBIUS: Name one at a time.
               I'll tell each fate in turn.

HECUBA: Cassandra first, my daughter:

TALTHYBIUS: Daughter of grief. Whose... lot was she?
                Lord Agamemnon's:
                Selected, not allotted.

HECUBA: To be Clytemnestra's slave.
                Omee mee.

TALTHYBIUS: To be his majesty's bedmate,
                His concubine.

HECUBA: Apollo's virgin? Eternal chastity
                Her gift from the gold-haired god!

TALTHYBIUS: Divine possession.
                To... possess that... fired the king.

HECUBA: Your garlands, child,
                Your crown, your laurels:
                Strip them, hurl them down.

TALTHYBIUS: It's no light honour
                To share a prince's bed.

HECUBA: My youngest child,
                My chick you stole,
                Where, where?

TALTHYBIUS: Polyxena, you mean?

HECUBA: Whose... luck was she?

TALTHYBIUS: She... tends Achilles' tomb.
                It was decreed.

HECUBA: Oee moee.
                My daughter, a tomb-attendant!
                What justice, sir, is this?

TALTHYBIUS: Be glad for her.
Your daughter's pain is done.

HECUBA: What d'you mean?
She's still alive? She sees the Sun?

TALTHYBIUS: Her destiny cradles her.
Her pain is done.

HECUBA: And Hector's wife, our warlord's wife?
Unhappy Andromache, what of her?

TALTHYBIUS: Prince Neoptolemus chose her.
A royal prize.

HECUBA: And what of me? Tottering...
Propped on a stick... whose slave am I?

TALTHYBIUS: Lord Odysseus of Ithaca has chosen you.

HECUBA: E! E!
Tear your shorn head,
Rake your cheeks.
Eeoh meemee!
To be that man's slave.
I spit on him,
Deceiver, monster, liar.
True, false, love, hate,
He twists them,
Writhes, the serpent tongue.
Weep for me, women:
Weep for your queen defiled,
Debased, destroyed.

Music ends. From this point, all speak.

CHORUS: Majesty, you know your fate.

	But mine? Which Greek owns mine?

TALTHYBIUS: *(to Attendants)*
Go in, now. Fetch Cassandra.
Leave the rest to me.
I'll put her in Agamemnon's hands,
And distribute the others,
Each to her man.
Ha! Fire, inside. What is it?
The prisoners - torching their quarters,
Setting themselves on fire?
Death before exile?
Is that what they choose - free spirits
Refusing to face disaster?
Open the gates! Hurry!
I'll not be blamed for this.

HECUBA: Be quiet. There's no fire,
No burning. It's Cassandra my daughter,
Running, gripped by god.

Music. Enter Cassandra with blazing torches.

CASSANDRA: Bring the torch. Shine it   [*strophe*]
Here, here,
Light this holy place.
Hymen! Oh!
Blessed is the groom,
The bride,
Cassandra, blessed,
Married in Argos.
Hymen! Oh!

Mother? Weeping? For father,
For fatherland?
See me lift the torch,
See, see, it flowers,
Fire flowers
For Hymen,

For Hecate,
Marriage-gods,
I honour them.

Dance with me. Dance,   [*antistrophe*]
Be happy,
Dance as we danced for father,
King of kings.
Lord Apollo, dance with us,
Lead us.
In your temple, laurel-crowned,
For you, this sacrifice.
Hymen! Oh!

Mother, dance, lead the dance.
Like this, like this,
Twirling, leaping, look.
Sing wedding songs,
Cry joy,
Cry blessings. Women,
Put on your finery,
Sing my song, my husband's song,
My destiny.

Music ends.

CHORUS: Can't you stop her, Majesty?
She's entranced.
She'll be in the Greek camp,
Head over heels, before she knows it.

HECUBA: God of fire, at weddings
You light the torch, set hearts aflame.
But here you kindle misery,
Far from my hopes.
Cassandra, child, I planned
Such a different wedding-day: not here

At the point of sharp Greek spears.
Give me the torch.
You're not holding it straight. Be calm.
You need your wits about you now.
Hush. Take the torches, women.
She'll stop. No more wedding songs.
It's time for tears.

CASSANDRA: Rejoice, mother.
Crown me with flowers. I've won.
I'm marrying a king. Take me to him;
Make me, give me no choice.
Trust Apollo. If God is god,
This marriage will ruin His Lordship.
Agamemnon, grand admiral of Greece!
I'll hurt him more than Helen did.
I'll kill him, strip all his house
Till the price is paid
For my father and brothers dead.
Cassandra, hush! Don't tell it all:
Don't sing of knives, necks chopped,
Mine and those others',
Blood-feud, the mother dead,
The dynasty destroyed.
My marriage-price!
Sane now, no madness,
I tell you this: God's words.
We outrank the Greeks. We win.
What did they do?
For one woman's sake, one fuck,
They hunted Helen,
Squandered a million lives.
Agamemnon -
So experienced, so worldly-wise -
Killed what he loved for what he hated,
Threw away happiness, children, home,
For his brother's woman,

The wife who left
Of her own free choice,
Whom no one forced.
So they flocked to the Scamander,
Lined up to die
On a foreign river's banks,
On a foreign plain -
For what? Their city?
The towers of their native land?
Plucked, they'll never see
Their children; their wives' soft hands
Won't sheet them for burial.
They sleep in foreign soil.
And what of those at home?
Widows, fathers stripped of their sons,
They die alone. Who weeps for them?
Whose offerings drench their tombs?

Now, what of Troy?
What of our Trojans, dead
For their native land?
What more could they ask?
Spears snatched them. Loving hands,
Friends' hands, carried them home,
Made them decent for burial.
The earth of Troy enfolds them.
Others escaped, day after day escaped,
To smile on their wives, their children.
What Greek had that?
Is it Hector you weep for,
His cruel death? I tell you, no other man
Ever died so rich in reputation –
And that was the gift of Greeks.
If they'd stayed at home,
Who now would know his name?
And Paris. He could have married
A nobody, a name on no one's lips.
Instead: Helen of Sparta,

Daughter of Zeus on high.
If wars must be fought,
A glorious death, not a coward's,
Brings honour to the city.
You see? Mother? Don't weep for Troy.
Don't weep for me.
Your enemies, my enemies -
I'll marry, and destroy them all.

CHORUS: You talk in riddles. You're stripped
               Of everything but misery - and laugh.

TALTHYBIUS: Lord Apollo's snatched your wits, or else
               You'd pay for such prophecies of doom,
               Such omens as their majesties set sail.
               There's madness in the air; it touches us
               Equally, commoners and lords alike.
               High rank, high honour: no protection.
               Agamemnon for instance,
               Agamemnon son of Atreus,
               Commander-in-chief of Greece,
               Falls head over heels
               For you, a madwoman, a crazy one
               No nobody like me would bed.
               As for all this talk
               Of honest Troy, ignoble Greece:
               Pure craziness. I toss it on the wind.
               Come to the ships,
               His lordship's glittering prize.

               (*to Hecuba*)
               Odysseus will come for you,
               Laertes' son. Go with him.
               Do as he says. His wife,
               Your mistress now, is kind and fair –
               Or so they say who came to Troy.

CASSANDRA: How the dog yaps!

And how we honour them,
The nobodies, the hated ones
Who scurry on errands
From state to state!
My mother will come
To Odysseus' house - you say.
What of Apollo's prophecy,
Whispered to me,
That she would die in Troy?
And more besides.
I'm ashamed: I'll not tell it now.
I'm sorry for Odysseus. He'll suffer, too.
He'll count my misery,
Troy's agony, pure gold
Beside what he has to bear.
Ten years, ten more, must pass,
Before he comes home at last, alone.
Charybdis' gulf he'll see,
The maw of rock,
Polyphemus who stalks the hills,
Gnaws human flesh,
Sea-witch Circe
Who magics men to swine,
Shipwreck, drug-lust, the lotus,
Cows sacred to the Sun, their blood
Screams out their agony, his shame.
He'll plough the pit of Hell,
And live to boast of it.
And when he sails home at last,
Fair winds,
He'll find more trouble waiting,
A cloud, a swarm.

   Music.

Enough! Why shoot my arrows,
My prophecies, at him? Lead the way.

Make a procession. To my marriage-bed
Of death. Agamemnon,
Lord, prince of dishonour,
Dishonourably you'll die.
You'll scrabble in the dark,
In deadly dark,
Who claim such glittering deeds.
Naked, sodden, they'll dump my corpse
For beasts to pick beside your grave,
Our marriage-bed. Apollo's drudge!
Off with you, garlands, love-tokens.
What ceremonies now? What banquets?
Go, go, flowers of my flesh,
The virgin speaks, fly free,
Find your master, wind's wings, Apollo!

Where's the ship, his lordship's ship?
I'm ready. Sniff the breeze, quick,
Wind kiss the sails.
Embark me, sail me away:
A Fury, one of three.
Smile goodbye, mother. Don't cry.
O Troy, beloved Troy,
My brothers, my father down below,
Be ready. I'll come to you,
Laughing, soon, tear down
That house of Atreus that toppled Troy,
And come to you.

Music ends. Talthybius leads her out.

CHORUS: The queen! Quickly!
The queen's fainted.
Some of you! Help her.
Don't leave her lying there.
For shame!

HECUBA: No, leave me. I'll lie where I am.
                 I want no help. Engulfed, overwhelmed -
                 What else should I do but faint?
                 O gods! Poor allies,
                 But who else, what else, is left?
                 I'll sing my former happiness once more:
                 How different, how pitiful,
                 What now I bear!
                 I was queen of Troy;
                 My husband king of kings,
                 My sons no rank and file
                 But princes, warlords.
                 What mother in Troy, in Greece,
                 In all the world, could boast such sons?
                 One by one
                 I watched Greeks harvest them.
                 I chopped my hair for them,
                 Wept at their tombs. I wept for Priam,
                 Who sowed them, with these own eyes
                 Saw him sliced to death at the altar fire.
                 Saw my city raped. My daughters,
                 Reared to make royal marriages,
                 Reared by these hands,
                 I saw them snatched away.
                 Shall I see them again? Will they see me?
                 My future's built for me: a wall, a cell.
                 I'm to go to Greece,
                 An old woman, a slave;
                 I'm to do what I'm told,
                 Whatever they decide.
                 Hector's mother! Shall I keep the door?
                 Bake bread? Stretch out in the dust,
                 Ragged body, ragged clothes,
                 Who once wore silk,
                 Who shared the royal bed?
                 Oee, what a change is here! For her sake,
                 That woman's sake,
                 That I be brought to this!

Cassandra, you danced,
You spoke with gods -
Now your honour's
Like water in your hands.
Polyxena, little one, where are you?
So many little ones, sons, daughters -
Who'll hold me now, who'll comfort me?
Why pick me up?
What d'you want of me?
I once walked proud in Troy. No more!
Lead me to slavery.
Straw bed, stone pillow.
I'll lie in misery, I'll weep my life away.
Princes! So fortunate!
Call none of us lucky before we die.

Music.

CHORUS: My song is a song of Troy,   [*strophe*]
               New song, death song,
               Song of grief for Troy.
               Then we died,
               Spear-booty, died,
               When that four-wheeled beast
               Faced gates of Troy,
               Gold-chink, spear-roar,
               Greek spears that filled the sky.
               High on the heights
               Our people cried,
               'Troy's wars are done!
               Fetch it inside, the wonder,
               Offer it, give it to Our Lady Athene,
               Daughter of Zeus on high.'
               So they sang, they ran,
               Girls, old women,
               Shouting for joy,
               Tricked, doomed.

They swarmed to the gates,   [*antistrophe*]
Whole generations,
The seed of Troy.
They dragged it -
Pine, polished, womb of Greeks -
To offer it in Athene's shrine,
Virgin lady who loves the horse.
Like a ship, dark-hulled,
Woven ropes bound tight,
It swam through Troy
Till they moored it on temple floor:
Stone anchorage, the death of Troy.
Night fell. Darkness.
Whistle of flutes,
Beat of dancing feet:
Troy's maidens danced and sang.
Torches in every house
Scattered the darkness,
Flickered in sleep.

I was in the palace,
Dancing, shouting Athene's name,
Virgin daughter of Zeus
Who treads the peaks.
A shout of blood
Through the city.
Children, little ones,
Cling to their mothers,
Trembling. Ares the wargod
Bursts from that wooden womb,
Swaggers down every street.
Blood steams on our altars,
Men's blood, the blood of Troy.
Girls, widows, groan in our beds,
Seedbed of baby Greeks,
Seedbed of tears for Troy.

Music ends. Attendants bring in Andromache, in
a cart loaded with booty. Her baby Astyanax is in
her arms.

Hecuba, look: Andromache.
Sobbing, there in that cart.
Astyanax cradled in her arms,
Lord Hector's son, her darling.
Lady, poor lady,
Where are they carting you,
With all the other spoils,
Spearspoils, gold, bronze
Looted from Troy by Achilles' son
To hang in temples of the Greeks?

Music.

ANDROMACHE: Our lords the Greeks are taking me.

HECUBA: Oee moee.

ANDROMACHE: Weep now, as I weep.

HECUBA: Aee aee.

ANDROMACHE: Pain.

HECUBA: O Zeus.

ANDROMACHE: Disaster.

HECUBA: Children.

ANDROMACHE: No more.

HECUBA: Troy's majesty, gone.

ANDROMACHE: Weep.

HECUBA: My children, gone.

ANDROMACHE: Weep, weep.

HECUBA: Weep for me.

ANDROMACHE: Weep tears.

HECUBA: Weep for Troy.

ANDROMACHE: Our Troy.

HECUBA: Ashes.

ANDROMACHE: Hector, husband.

HECUBA: Poor child, he's dead:
My son, your husband.

ANDROMACHE: Be strong for me.
Greek-slayer -

HECUBA: My firstborn,
Priam's heir -

ANDROMACHE: Let me die with you,
Let me lie with you.

HECUBA: How can we bear it?

ANDROMACHE: Our city, gone.

HECUBA: Pain piled on pain.

ANDROMACHE: God's fault. Your son's fault. Paris,
Your son, my brother. You let him live;
He slept with that woman,

And toppled Troy.
Red corpses he piled at Athene's feet,
Vultures' meat. He yoked us. Slaves!

HECUBA: Troy, mother Troy.

ANDROMACHE: I weep for you. I leave you.

HECUBA: You know your fate.

ANDROMACHE: I weep for home, for childbed.

HECUBA: Children, your mother's torn from you,
Torn from her city. Tears in the house,
Our house is a sea of tears.
Only the dead live free of pain.

Music ends.

CHORUS: Tears in trouble: sweet solace,
Shared misery, the muse of pain.

ANDROMACHE: D'you see this, mother?
Your son was Hector, Greek-slayer.
D'you see this now?

HECUBA: I see gods' work.
They pile high towers of nothing;
They tumble what we think great.

ANDROMACHE: War-booty. They're parceling us away,
My child and I.
We're princes, and look: we're slaves.

HECUBA: Fate treads us down. They came
Just now to snatch Cassandra.
Gone: no choice.

ANDROMACHE: Feoo feoo.
                She was stolen before,
                Dragged from the shrine -
                Now a second outrage.
                And there's more to bear.

HECUBA: Who'll count my misery? Who'll end it?
                Pain races pain. They make a game of it.

ANDROMACHE: Your daughter's dead. Polyxena.
                They cut her throat,
                To drench Achilles' grave.

HECUBA: Oee! Talthybius' riddle - clear at last!

ANDROMACHE: I saw her. I climbed from the cart;
                I covered her; I beat my breast for her.

HECUBA: Aee aee. Polyxena, child, I weep for you.
                Human sacrifice, unjust.

ANDROMACHE: She's dead. It's done. She's lucky now.
                Far luckier than me. They make me live.

HECUBA: You're wrong, child.
                To put death before life!
                Death's emptiness. To live is hope.

ANDROMACHE: Mother, listen. Be comforted.
                When we die, it's like never being born,
                Far better than living
                On hands and knees. Who suffers
                After death? Who still feels pain?
                To fall from wealth, from power - to fall,
                Live on, remember -
                That racks the mind. She's dead.
                It's as if she'd never seen the Sun.

Her suffering's forgotten. Gone.
But I! I bent my bow at happiness.
I hit the target. Hit, and hit - and missed.
I was Hector's wife. I kept my place,
Did my duty, stayed indoors
As women should. No loose talk,
No market chatter. All I knew
I learned from my own quiet thoughts,
At home. When Hector spoke,
I listened. Downcast eyes. I knew
When to let him have his way,
When to insist. My reputation spread,
Through all the Greeks -
And brought me this.
As soon as the city fell,
As soon as I was taken,
Achilles' son chose me for consort.
I'm to serve as slave
In the house of the man
Who killed my husband. What shall I do?
Blot out my Hector's face, fling wide
My heart to a second husband -
And betray the dead?
Or scorn Achilles' son,
Pull down my master's rage
About my head? One night of love
Unstrings a woman's hate,
Makes her dote on the man she loathed.
Men say.
Men say.
I spit on wives who transfer their love,
Take it handy from bed to bed.
Even a horse,
Removed from its stable-mate,
Rejects the yoke.
A dumb, wild beast,
Unreasoning, so much less than human!

Hector, you were all I asked:
Brave, noble, kind.
You married me unblemished
From my father's house; I gave you
My virginity. Now you're dead.
I'm to sail away to Greece,
A prisoner of war, a slave. See, mother,
Polyxena's death,
The death you weep for,
Is nothing beside what I must bear, alive.
I've nothing, not even that seed of hope
They say lives in everyone.
I'd like to think I'll be happy.
I'm not such a fool. I won't.

CHORUS: You suffer as we suffer. Your words
       Remind us how deep in grief we stand.

HECUBA: I've never been on a ship.
       I've seen them in paintings;
       I've heard people talk of them.
       When the sea's calm, winds blow fair,
       The crew stay easily in control:
       One steers, one trims the sail, one bails.
       But when storms blow, seas howl,
       They throw up their hands
       And roll with fate.
       So it is with me. Trouble swamps me.
       I roll with the gods. I bite my lip.
       Andromache, child, let Hector be:
       Your tears can't help him now.
       Your new master: honour him, obey him,
       Snare his affection. You'll help us all,
       Your loved ones; you'll keep your son;
       You'll bring him up - and one day,
       God send it so,
       His descendants will come to Troy,
       Will settle here. Our city will live again.

Look: something else. He's here,
That runner of the Greeks. More news.

Enter Talthybius.

TALTHYBIUS: My lady, noble wife of noble Hector,
I come unwillingly. Don't blame me.
I bring a unanimous decree:
Agamemnon, Menelaus, the other lords,
I speak their words.

ANDROMACHE: What is it? You begin so carefully...

TALTHYBIUS: Your son... How can I say it?

ANDROMACHE: Different masters? They're separating us?

TALTHYBIUS: No Greek will own this child.

ANDROMACHE: He's to stay here, last trace of Troy?

TALTHYBIUS: There's no good way
To tell the news I bring.

ANDROMACHE: Such reluctance.
What is it? Some disaster?

TALTHYBIUS: They've condemned your son to die.

ANDROMACHE: Oee moee.
Marriage I could bear. Not this.

TALTHYBIUS: Odysseus' plan, but every lord agreed.

ANDROMACHE: Aee aee, aee aee.
Beyond all bearing. Pain.

TALTHYBIUS: No hero's son, he said, should thrive.

ANDROMACHE: His own sons too. Let them not... thrive.

TALTHYBIUS: He's to be dashed
From the highest tower.
Give way, lady.
Be wise. Give up your son.
Shed royal tears, show dignity,
But give him up. You can't prevent it.
Your power has gone,
Your city, your husband.
We do as we like. You're ours.
One woman: we're strong enough!
Don't fight us. Don't resist.
Do nothing rash.
Provoke us, your son won't die... easily,
Won't lie in a grave.
Take my advice. Accept.
You'll earn him burial, yourself...
Respect.

ANDROMACHE: Poor little boy. We loved you so.
We were so proud of you.
Our enemies want to kill you,
To tear your mother's heart.
Your father was a prince.
How did that help you?
It brought you this. Why, Hector?
Did I marry you, come here to Troy,
To our marriage-bed - for this?
My son was to rule all Asia,
Not be blood-sacrifice - for Greeks!
Don't cry, darling.
D'you understand what's happening?
You're holding me, clutching me.
Who'll rescue you? Not Hector,

Spear springing from the grave.
Not his brothers, the might of Troy.
You'll fall, break your neck,
Life gone. They'll watch dry-eyed.
Poor baby. Let me hug you tight.
How sweet you smell. Was it for this
I writhed in childbirth, wrapped you,
Gave you my breast to suck - for this?
Hold me, darling. Kiss me. Say goodbye.
Greeks!
You count yourselves so civilised -
And this is what you do!
An innocent child. Why kill him?
Helen, daughter of Zeus they call you,
But I give you other fathers:
Demons, grudges, blood-lust, death,
Every foulness that sprouts in Earth.
How did Zeus ever father you,
Snail-slime to Greece, to Troy,
To all the world?
You glanced our way, those pretty eyes,
Smeared us with death.
The plains of Troy!
Take him. Throw him. Drink his blood.
God speaks; my case is heard;
I'm to let my own son die.
Take me to the ship.
I'm to marry a prince,
But first, I'm to lose my child.

CHORUS: Unhappy Troy, destroyed - for Helen,
            That woman, that marriage, cursed.

            Music. Talthybius takes Astyanax.

TALTHYBIUS: Come, boy,
            Away from your mother's arms.

Up to the battlements,
That crown of towers.
Snuff out your life: it's decreed.
Take him. Who could bring such news
Without pity, without embarrassment?
Whose heart is so hard? Not mine.

Exit, followed by Attendants, with Astyanax.
Andromache is wheeled out on her cart.

HECUBA: Child, child of my child of tears,
They're robbing us,
Stealing your life from us. Why?
Poor child. What can I do?
Beat head, beat breast, that's all.
Oee! Troy! Child!
We're hurtling to disaster -
What's left for us?

CHORUS: See how they came to Troy: [*strophe*]
King Telamon of Salamis,
Its waves, its buzz of bees,
Island leaning in to land,
To that sacred slope
Where grey-eyed Athene first
Grey-green olives grew,
Crown on glittering crown
For Athens, her city, her people.
From Salamis king Telamon
Marched with Heracles, Alcmena's son,
Kings twinned in bravery,
To Troy, to Troy,
That once was ours.

See how they came to Troy: [*antistrophe*]
Heracles, the flower of Greece.
To Simois, its mudflats, its shallows;
Shipped oars, made fast,
Took from its place the bow,

Strung death for Laomedon,
King of Troy, who cheated him.
Hewn stone, true to the line,
Apollo's work, he smashed,
Burned; fire, red fire,
Laid waste the land of Troy.
Beat, beat against the walls,
Spearpoints, blood-drops,
The blood of Troy.

In vain now Ganymede,   [*strophe*]
Once prince of Troy,
Snatched to heaven,
Cupbearer to gods,
In vain your pride,
Stepping up to Zeus,
Bowing low to Zeus,
Filling golden cup, so proud:
Your motherland burns.
Her beaches booming, howling,
Shriek for chicks forlorn,
Mothers for children,
Wives for husbands,
Grannies, gone.
Your running-place,
The pool you bathed in -
How can you stand by Zeus' throne,
And smile? Troy's gone.

In vain now Love   [*antistrophe*]
Brought gods to Troy,
Filled all their thoughts,
Built towers,
Troy towering in their hearts.
Zeus, Ganymede; Tithonus, Dawn;
The gods and Troy, at one.
Yet what was that to Zeus,
To white-winged Dawn,

Whose lovely light
Gazed on the death of Troy,
Unmoved, who took from this land
Tithonus, husband,
Child-sower,
Snatched him high in golden chariot,
Four horses, high to the stars,
Hope of his native land? In vain!
Gods' love is dead in Troy.

Music ends. Enter Menelaus.

MENELAUS: Bright sunshine! Happy day,
When Menelaus lays hands on...
Her again.
To suffer so, for such a wife!
They think I came to Troy for her.
Not so. I came for him,
That guest no-guest
Who lodged in my palace
And stole my wife.
The price is paid, God saw to that:
That man and his country,
By Greek spears dead.
Now I come for her, the Spartan -
I still can't speak her name and smile.
She's mine, tagged here
With all the other spoil.
The men who risked their lives for her
Have handed her to me.
I can kill her here or ship her home.
Helen! Hell to her native land!
I'll cargo her home
To death, to pay the price
For so many friends,
So many loved ones, lost.
Bring her out here. Drag her: that hair,

Scabbed with dead men's blood.
As soon as the winds blow fair,
We'll take her home.

HECUBA: O Zeus, who sustains, who rules,
          Zeus of many names, invisible,
          Unimaginable, power of nature,
          Breath of thought, Zeus, hear me.
          You walk the secret paths,
          Your justice guides –

MENELAUS: What prayers are these?

HECUBA: My lord, you plan to kill your wife.
          But don't look at her, face to face.
          Lust, lust, she steals men's eyes;
          Cities fall, houses blaze for her.
          Seduction. You, I, the dead all know.

          Enter Helen, guarded.

HELEN: Menelaus, what's happening?
          I'm frightened.
          Your men lay hands on me.
          Do you hate me so?
          Even so, I'll ask.
          What have you decided,
          You and their lordships?
          Must I live, or die?

MENELAUS: No public decision.
          It was me you wronged.
          They gave you to me to kill.

HELEN: May I speak? Make my appeal?
          I'll show you: I don't deserve to die.

MENELAUS: No words. I want your death.

HECUBA: Lord, let her speak -
                   And let me answer.
                   You don't know how she was in Troy.
                   I'll tell you what she did.
                   Don't worry: the tale means death.

MENELAUS: Time-wasting. But if she must, she must.
                   It's granted - but for your sake, not hers.
                   I owe her no favours. That's understood.

HELEN: You think I'm your enemy.
                   Good arguments or bad,
                   You won't discuss with me,
                   Not face to face. Never mind.
                   I'll imagine your part, your charges,
                   And I'll answer them one by one.
                   She began it, began disaster, giving birth
                   To Paris - the firebrand, the torch
                   She dreamt would topple Troy.
                   Her husband, his ancient majesty,
                   Changed the baby's name,
                   Let 'Alexander' live -
                   Disaster for Troy, for me.
                   Hear what happened next.
                   Three goddesses appeared,
                   Asked Paris to judge between them.
                   'Choose me,' Athene said,
                   'And your armies will sack great Greece.'
                   'Choose me,' said Hera, 'And all Asia,
                   All Europe, will be yours.'
                   Aphrodite next.
                   She admired my beauty, promised me
                   To Paris - as soon as she won the prize.
                   She won - and all that followed,
                   All I and Paris did,
                   Was to benefit Greece, not Troy.

Is it you that strangers rule, spearlords
From overseas? Greece rose; I fell.
I should be wearing a victor's crown.
Instead, I'm sold for my beauty,
Spat upon.

What do you answer?
'That's not the point. You betrayed
Your husband, slipped away.'
When Alexander, Paris,
However you name him -
When that criminal, her son, arrived,
A most powerful goddess
Was at his side - and you left him
Behind at home, you fool,
While you sailed to Crete
On business! Well.
Next I question myself, not you.
What was I thinking of? Why did I go
With him, a stranger, leave home,
Betray my friends, my country?
My answer: punish her,
Punish Aphrodite.
Her power rules even Zeus.
How could I resist?

What else? Another charge?
When Paris was killed,
When he plunged to Hell, our union,
Ordained by gods, was over. You'll say
I should have left Troy's palace then,
Run to your ships. I tried.
They'll tell you,
Gate-keepers, sentries, tower-guards,
Forever catching me
As I tried to slip away,
As I lowered myself
From the battlements on ropes.

Menelaus, husband, can you kill me?
It's unjust. He made me sleep with him;
Everything I was enslaved me;
How could I win? The gods
Did this. Do you challenge
Their will, their power?
Are you so foolish?

CHORUS: Majesty, break through this spell,
Defend your people, your children.
Fine words, foul deeds:
She knows them all.

HECUBA: First, for the goddesses:
I take their part. She's lying.
What, Hera, queen of Heaven,
Pallas Athene, so beside themselves
That one offers Argos to barbarians,
The other Athens?
That they come to Troy
For a beauty contest, a childish game?
Why should Hera fret about her looks -
To find a husband surpassing Zeus?
Why should Athene look for marriage
Among the gods - Athene, who shuns
The marriage bed, who begged
Eternal virginity from her father, Zeus?
Don't gloss your crime
By calling goddesses fools.
We know what you're doing.
We understand.
Most ridiculous of all, you claim
That Aphrodite went with my son
To Sparta. Why should she?
She could have sat where she was,
In Olympus, and carried all Sparta,
Every one of you, to Troy.

As soon as you saw my son,
My handsome son,
You flared with lust. Melted.
It's human. He dazzled you:
His robes, his gold. You licked your lips.
How cheap your Sparta seemed!
In Troy
You could riot and reel in wealth.
Menelaus' palace -
How could you wallow,
Gorge yourself on gold, in that?
You say my son forced you,
Dragged you away. Who saw?
Who heard you shout for help?
Castor was there, your brother;
Pollux, too -
Human princes still, not yet made stars.
Then, when the Greeks pelted after you
To Troy, when the struggle,
The storm of spears, began,
If Menelaus won the slightest victory
You needled my son:
What a man his rival was! But if
The Trojans were successful, nothing.
You made yourself fate's weathervane.
Duty, loyalty, were words unknown.
Woven ropes, you say?
You let yourself down
From the battlements on ropes?
You longed to leave? Who saw you
Twisting a noose, sharpening a dagger -
As any princess of honour,
Wife, would have done,
Missing her former husband?
I said to you, often: 'Daughter, go.
My sons will find other wives.
I'll show you secret ways

To the Greek ships. End the war,
For Greece, for us.' How you frowned!
No more queening it in Paris' house,
No barbarians kissing the ground
You walked on. You lived for that.
Now you come out here, in that dress,
You breathe this air - with him,
Your husband? I spit on you.
Wear rags, shave your head,
Weep tears of shame
After what you did. Not this!
I've done, Menelaus. Kill her.
For you, for Greece!
Let her death teach all unfaithful wives.

CHORUS: Kill her, Menelaus. Your ancestors,
               Your royal house, demand it.
               Greeks call you a coward, a woman:
               Prove them wrong
               By what you do here, today.

MENELAUS: I agree with you. She chose it.
               She went to that stranger's bed
               Of her own free will.
               She blames Aphrodite -
               Nonsense! Go.
               They're waiting to stone you.
               Pay for my disgrace,
               For ten long years of war.

HELEN: I'm on my knees.
               God's fault, not mine.
               Don't kill me. Spare me.

HECUBA: Remember your friends,
               Your allies, their children,
               Dead for her.
               In all their names, I beg you -

MENELAUS: Enough, old woman. I'm ignoring her.
            I'm giving the orders.
            She'll be shipped aboard,
            Be cargoed home.

HECUBA: Not in your ship!

MENELAUS: Why not? She's put on weight?

HECUBA: Lust, lord. It never dies.

MENELAUS: That depends who lusts.
            Still, as you wish. It's reasonable.
            A different ship. And when she's home,
            A dishonourable death
            To match her life, to show
            All women what duty means. Hard –
            But a lesson they all must learn,
            Even the stupid ones, even those
            More shameless than she is.
            She dies; they learn.

            Exit. Helen is led out. Music.

CHORUS: Lord Zeus, you betrayed us,   [*strophe*]
            Gave Greek enemies our shrines,
            Our altars, flame of sacrifice,
            Smoke pluming the sky, incense,
            Holy Pergamum, Mount Ida,
            Ivy-groves, snow-swollen streams,
            Dawn pointing on the peaks,
            Radiant, blessed, benign.

            Gone now sacrifice, choir-songs,   [*antistrophe*]
            Night-festivals in honour of the gods,
            Dancing, gods of beaten gold,
            Twelve gods of Troy, sweet sacrifice,

Moon-cakes altar-burned to honour you.
Lord of lords, look down,
From your throne look down,
Take heed of my city, slain.

Darling husband, dead,   [*strophe*]
You wander unburied,
No offerings poured.
Ships wing us to Argos,
The castle, high walls,
Green meadows where horses graze.
Our children throng the gates,
Weeping, crying.
'Mother, they snatch us,
Snatch us from your arms,
Your eyes, to Salamis,
Its temples,
To Corinth,
Pelops' palace,
Isthmus between two seas.'

While Menelaus sails   [*antistrophe*]
Let lightning flare,
Hurled by hand of Zeus,
Smash oars, smash oars.
From Troy he drags me, full of tears,
To slavery, far away, while she,
Daughter of Zeus,
Preens herself in golden mirrors,
Laughs. Sink him far from home,
From Sparta, hearth and home,
Kill her, his prize,
Who shamed great Greece,
Wed Paris,
Wed misery,
Grief and agony for Troy.

Enter Talthybius, with Attendants carrying the
body of Astyanax, laid on the shield of his father
Hector.

CHORUS:　　　　Eeoh, eeoh.
New anguish, pain on pain.
Look, women: Astyanax.
They murdered him,
Tossed him like a toy
From the city walls.

Music ends.

TALTHYBIUS:　　Hecuba, one galley waits,
Riding at anchor, ready to take
Neoptolemus' last warspoils
Home to his rocky land. My lord himself
Long since set sail: bad news from home,
Unrest in the palace, hurried him away.
He took Andromache.
She wept for Troy, for Hector, gone.
She begged Neoptolemus
To bury these remains: her son,
Your Hector's son, who lost his life
When he fell from the battlements.
Tears filled my eyes. This shield -
Bronze-ribbed, terror of Greeks,
Lord Hector's wall in war:
She begged it from the spoils,
Begged Neoptolemus
Not to hang it
As a trophy on his bedroom wall,
But to bury the child on it, here in Troy.
No sarcophagus of wood or stone.
We were to bring him to you,
To hold, wrap, crown for burial
As best you can, as things now are.

Her lord was hurrying her away;
She had no time. See to it, then:
Make him ready.
We'll bury him, and sail.
No time to waste.
I saved you one sad task:
As I crossed the river to come here,
I washed him and cleaned the wounds.
Now I'll dig a grave. If we work
As fast as we can, each of us,
We'll soon sail home.

Exit.

HECUBA: Put down the shield, my Hector's shield.
I should smile to see it; it tears my heart.
O Greeks, how big you are, how brave!
Why murder him? A child!
Were you afraid?
That he'd pile up Troy again,
Make it great again? We're dead.
We were dying even then,
When Hector swam
In his glory, in all that sea of spears.
We were dying even then –
A million men! –
And now our city's gone.
You're afraid of one tiny child.
It's beyond belief: I spit on you.
My little one, why did you die like this?
You could have died for Troy,
A grown man, a husband,
In majesty like the gods:
Fulfilled, if such things bring fulfilment.
Your inheritance! You saw it every day,
You knew it in your heart,
And it's snatched away.
Poor little boy. Your curls, your mother

Kissed them, tended them,
Flowers in a garden.
Now they're ripped away:
The hard stones,
Troy's stones, Apollo's stones.
Blood grins in broken bone.
How can I bear it?
Such sweet hands, your father's hands,
Dangling. Lips, dear lips.
How they chattered,
What promises they made.
D'you remember? How you hugged me?
'Granny, when you die
I'll cut off all my hair.
I'll come to your grave
With all my friends.
We'll sing and sing for you.' Not so.
Old buries young.
A child; an old woman,
Cityless. Oee moee.
Were they for this,
Hugs, kisses,
Sleepless nights
When I watched you sleep?
What can we write of you,
Write on your tomb?
'This baby scared the Greeks.
They murdered him.'
Hear that in Greece, and blush!
Your father's power and wealth,
They're not for you.
Your inheritance is one bronze shield,
Your bed below the earth. His shield,
Your father's shield. It kept him safe;
He gripped it close; his arm;
His handprint, here on the handle, sweat
Staining the polish,
Here where he leaned,

Sweat soaked his beard
In the battle-storm.

Bring what's there,
What you can, to wrap him.
Poor boy! We've nothing:
Fate sees to that.
But all we have is yours.
How mortals preen themselves.
Power! Wealth!
They're ours; they're gone;
Luck prances away.
If we're fooled by human happiness,
We're fools.

CHORUS: They're bringing cloaks, stripped
               From Trojan dead, to wrap him in.

HECUBA: These are for you, child. Not prizes
               For riding or shooting
               Among your friends, presented by
               Her majesty your grandmother.
               Your own pretty things, your inheritance,
               Looted by Helen, hated of the gods,
               Who stole your life,
               Laid waste your house.

                    Music.

CHORUS: E! E! Arrows in the heart!
               So great, so royal a prince.

HECUBA: *(spoken)*
               These robes are yours.
               Wedding robes, for your marriage
               To some princess from far away.
               Shield, glory of Hector,

Mother of victories,
Here is your crown.
Dead with this death,
You'll never die. He honours you.
What shield
Of Odysseus, so wise, so false,
Now shines so bright?

CHORUS: Aee aee, aee aee. Child of tears,
            Earth welcomes you. Weep, mother.

HECUBA: Aee aee, aee aee.

CHORUS: Weep for all the dead.

HECUBA: Oee moee.

CHORUS: Oee moee. No memory but tears.

HECUBA: (spoken)
            I bandage your wounds,
            A poor doctor who finds no cure.
            Your father will ease your pain
            There with the dead below.

CHORUS: Beat head. Row.
            Eeoh moee moee.

HECUBA: Women, friends –

CHORUS: What, lady?

HECUBA: (spoken)
            The gods planned this: my pain,
            My Troy, picked out to hate.
            We honoured them for nothing.
            Why did they do this, uproot the world?
            To make a myth of us,

Give poets a theme for plays?
Go, bury him. Such a little grave!
He's dressed, crowned,
For the world below.
He has what he has.
Fine clothes, riches -
They're toys for the living, boasts.
Who says the dead take heed of them?

CHORUS: Eeoh eeoh.
Mother of misery.
Hope shredded.
Noble father, noble son,
Destroyed, brought down.
Eah eah!

Music ends. Attendants take out Astyanax's body.

CHORUS: Look, there in the city.
Men, torches. Fire.
New misery.

Enter Talthybius, attended.

TALTHYBIUS: You know your orders. Burn the palace.
Flatten it. As soon as it's down,
We go. The day we've longed for. Home!
Women, these words are for you as well.
When the trumpet sounds, here in camp,
It's time to leave. Go to the ships.
Majesty, queen of grief, go now.
Go with these men
To Odysseus, your allotted lord.

HECUBA: Oee. What more must I bear?
My country, my city, burned.
Up, feet. Old woman, run.
Your city's dying.

Cherish it, say goodbye.
Troy! You breathed the breath of power,
You ruled all Asia,
Now they steal your name away.
They burn you. They drag us,
Exiles, slaves. Oh gods!
Why call on the gods -
Did they hear when we called before?
Into the fire. Die now,
Die here, with Troy.

*She runs towards the flames. Attendants restrain
her.*

TALTHYBIUS: Your suffering's made you mad.
Take her, quick. Odysseus' prize.

Music.

HECUBA: Otototoee.   [*strophe*]
Zeus,
Father, protector,
Do you see how they treat us?

CHORUS: He sees. Troy burns.
City of cities, uncitied now.

HECUBA: Otototoee.   [*antistrophe*]
Troy,
Blazing, toppling,
Do you see how it's burning?

CHORUS: Smoke, wings of smoke,
Our city speared, blown on the wind.

HECUBA: Earth of Troy,   [*strophe*]
You cradle them -

CHORUS: E! E!

HECUBA: D'you hear me, little ones? Your mother.

CHORUS: They're dead. You're crying to the dead.

HECUBA: I'll lie here, an old woman,
               On Mother Earth, I'll knock for them.

CHORUS: We'll kneel beside you,
               Call to our husbands
               There in the world below.

HECUBA: They're snatching us, taking us -

CHORUS: Hear her pain.

HECUBA: To be slaves, to the house of slaves.

CHORUS: Far from home, from Troy.

HECUBA: Eeoh eeoh. Priam. Dead.
               No grave. No friend.
               Do you see this now?

CHORUS: Death, darkness closed his eyes,
               Neat in that slaughterhouse.

HECUBA: Eeoh temples of gods,   [*antistrophe*]
               Beloved Troy.

CHORUS: E! E!

HECUBA: Blood-flame, spear-knives.

CHORUS: Dust to dust, forgotten.

HECUBA:	Ashes choke the sky. My people, my city, gone.
CHORUS:	Troy's dead. All gone. Away.
HECUBA:	Listen!
CHORUS:	Towers crash.
HECUBA:	Ground gapes.
CHORUS:	Engulfs.
HECUBA:	Eeoh eeoh. Up! Totter to slavery. It's time.
CHORUS:	Eeoh. Tears for Troy. Ships of Greece, we come.

Exeunt.

HECUBA

This translation of HECUBA was commissioned by the Gate Theatre, and was first performed there on 4 September 1992. The cast was as follows:

POLYDORUS...John Straiton
HECUBA...Ann Mitchell
POLYXENA...Sara Mair-Thomas
AGAMEMNON...Sylvester Morand
ODYSSEUS...Kevork Malikian
TALTHYBIUS...Christopher Robbie
POLYMESTOR...Don Warrington
CHORUS...........................Helen Anderson, Pamela Bennett, Elaine
                                Grant, Anna Healy, Ruth Lass, Sarah
                                Malin, Sara Markland, Helen Rimmer,
                                Chloe Thomas, Fiona Tong, Jayne
                                Trotman, Mary Woodvine
CHILDREN.....................................Jermaine Campbell and
                                    Jerome Campbell or Stephan
                                    Moses and Gavin Frazer
GUARDS............................Gary Williamson and Clive Cherrington

The play was directed by Laurence Boswell, and was designed by Stephen Brimson Lewis. Lighting design was by Jenny Kagan. The music was by Mick Sands, and the movement director was Christian Flint.

CHARACTERS

POLYDORUS' GHOST
HECUBA
POLYXENA
ODYSSEUS
TALTHYBIUS
AGAMEMNON
ATTENDANT
POLYMESTOR

SOLDIERS; POLYMESTOR'S SONS (silent parts)

CHORUS OF WOMEN

No-man's-land, before the ruins of Troy. Enter Polydorus' Ghost.

GHOST: You see Polydorus,
                 Son of Queen Hecuba,son of Priam.
                 From folds of the Underworld I come,
                 From gates of Night where Hades rules,
                 In exile from the gods.
                 I was a child, too young to shoulder arms
                 Or wear a sword. My father's city, Troy,
                 Was threatened by Greek might.
                 He sent me, in secret,
                 Here to Thrace, to an old ally,
                 Polymestor, who rules these farms,
                 These fields. These people breed horses.
                 Polymestor rules, their spear-lord.
                 So here I came, and with me
                 My father smuggled gold: if Troy fell,
                 His sons would still not starve.
                 So far, so good. Troy's towers survived.
                 My brother, Hector, kept his city safe.
                 I grew up here
                 In Thrace, at Polymestor's court,
                 Grew like a sapling - doomed.
                 Greeks snatch the life of Troy,
                 Snatch Hector's life, storm the palace,
                 Slaughter Priam my father
                 At his own altar.
                 Blood; butchery; Achilles' son.
                 News reaches Thrace.
                 My father's good old friend
                 Kills me for the gold, to keep the gold,
                 And dumps my carcass.
                 There on the shore I roll,
                 Roll on the tide-line, unwept, unburied.
                 Three days now.
                 My flesh an empty shell.
                 My spirit here, hovering.

My mother's here, unhappy Hecuba.
A prisoner-of-war in Thrace.
The whole Greek fleet sits here, waiting,
Here on these beaches.
They were dipping oars,
Stirring the sea for home,
When Achilles' ghost appeared,
There on his grave-mound,
Demanding, demanding
His share of honour, blood-sacrifice.
He demands Polyxena my sister,
Her life-blood. He'll get it.
They're his friends, they'll honour him.
My sister dies, today; it's fate.
And Hecuba? Two bodies,
Two children dead, she'll see,
My unhappy mother:
Polyxena's first, then mine.
They'll find me.
A slave-woman will find me,
Flotsam, sea-sodden; they'll bury me.
I begged this favour
From the powers below: a grave,
My own mother's hands to bury me.
It's granted, all I asked for, granted.

She's coming.
There, from Agamemnon's tent.
Old, afraid.
I appeared to her, she's terrified.
Feoo. Hecuba, how are you fallen!
Royal palace then,
The dust of slavery now.
Some god looked down on you,
Saw how high your pride,
And gave you this.

Exit. Music. Enter Hecuba, attended.

Hecuba: Help me, children. Here, outside.
                 Help the old woman, slave among slaves,
                 Who once was queen of Troy.
                 Your arm. Let me lean on you.
                 As fast as I can.

                 Light of day, darkness of night,
                 Terrors haunt me. Why?
                 Mother Earth, wing-beats, darkness:
                 Keep them away. Night-phantoms.
                 I saw, I saw.
                 Gods of the Underworld, keep him safe,
                 My son, our anchor, our future,
                 Safe in snowy Thrace.

                 Soon, soon:
                 More tears, eyes drowned in tears.
                 New grief. My heart shakes.
                 Where are they, Helenus, Cassandra,
                 My children, prophets,
                 To tell these dreams?

                 I saw a fawn.
                 Dappled. Torn from my lap.
                 Wolves' jaws. Blood. There,
                 Above the grave, Achilles' ghost,
                 Demanding, demanding,
                 Honour owed him,
                 Blood-sacrifice,
                 Woman's blood, royal blood.
                 O gods, deny these omens.
                 Keep my daughter safe.

                 Enter Chorus.

CHORUS: Hecuba, we hurried here.
                 Slaves, war-booty,
                 Agamemnon's share

Of spear-spoiled Troy,
From our master's tents
We hurried here, to tell you.
No good news. More pain.
We must tell you pain.
The Greeks, in full assembly,
It's decided: your daughter must die
To appease Achilles.
They were hoisting sail,
Ropes taut; his ghost appeared
In golden armour above his grave,
Crying 'Greeks!
Where are you going?
Will you leave my grave unhonoured?'
At once, among the spearmen,
A wave, a storm of argument.
'Sacrifice'. 'No sacrifice'.
Agamemnon took your side,
Hot for Cassandra,
The mad one, your daughter.
Against him, Theseus' sons,
Princes of Athens,
Gave different arguments
But the same advice:
Crown Achilles' grave
With fresh young blood.
'Achilles' fame' they said, 'Outranks
The pleasures of Cassandra's bed.'
Tense argument, word tug-of-war.
Then Odysseus stepped up,
Subtle Odysseus.
Crowd-charmer. Honey-tongue.
They fawned on him;
They drank his words.
'Will you spurn
The bravest of all the Greeks
To save a slave?

When our dead face Persephone,
There in the Underworld,
Must they look her in the eye and say
That their comrades ignored them,
Did them no honour
As they slipped from Troy?
Let me go, now. I'll fetch her.
The mother's old: trembling hands.
I'll snatch that child.'
Go to the temple, the altar,
Pray to gods above, below.
Only prayers can stop this,
Stop them tearing your child away,
Stop you watching
As she slumps on the grave,
Gold necklace purpling with blood
On white young throat.

    Music.

HECUBA: Oee. Heart breaks.   *[strophe]*
No words. No tears.
Wretched. Wretched.
Old woman. Slave.
O moee, moee.
Who'll protect me now?
City, Priam, sons, all gone.
Where, now, where?
Who'll save me?
The gods? The gods?
Women, this news, this pain,
I'm dead. Life gone.

Up. In. Go to her.
Weary. Go to her.
Polyxena, child, come out.
Hear your mother's tears.

Eeoh child.

Music ends. Enter Polyxena. [In what follows, in the original, she spoke while Hecuba sang.]

POLYXENA: Mother, mother, what is it?
Such cries. You scare me,
Like bird from bush. I'm here.

HECUBA: Oee, moee. Child.

POLYXENA: What's happened? I'm afraid.

HECUBA: Aee, aee. Your life.

POLYXENA: Mother, tell me. Don't hide it.
I'm frightened. Don't cry.
Mummy.

HECUBA: My child. My child. Disaster.

POLYXENA: What is it? Speak.

HECUBA: The Greeks, in council, unanimous.
Your death. Achilles' grave.

POLYXENA: Oee, moee. Horrible.
Horrible. Mummy.
Tell me. Tell me.

HECUBA: They say, they say...
The Greeks, your death,
It's settled.

[From this point, in the original, Polyxena also sang.]

POLYXENA: Oee. Mother.   *[antistrophe]*

Your grief. Your pain.
Outrage. Outrage.
Which god? Which?
What's left for you now?
Who'll share your pain,
Your slavery, old age?
I'm a calf,
Mountain calf, torn
From mother's side,
Throat cut, dark earth, down, down.
Nothing left. Weep, weep.

Music ends.

CHORUS: Look, Hecuba: Odysseus.
           Hurrying, with news.

Enter Odysseus.

ODYSSEUS: Woman. I think you know.
           It's decided. Voted.
           In plain words,
           The Greeks will sacrifice Polyxena,
           Your daughter,
           On Achilles' high-heaped grave.
           I'm here to fetch her. By order.
           Achilles' son, Neoptolemus,
           Will see to the sacrifice.
           It's decided. Your part is clear.
           No struggling. No pulling her back.
           We don't want you dragged from her.
           Accept the situation:
           Your helplessness, the need for dignity,
           Even when all is lost.

HECUBA: Aee aee.
           I come to the test. Strength. Misery.
           I should have died then. Before.

Zeus, why did you spare me,
For this, for this?
They tread on each other's heels.
Pain treads on pain.
Lord Odysseus, listen.
A free man, a slave - but listen.
I'll not offend you, not insult you.
Let me ask one question.
Then answer me.

ODYSSEUS: It's permitted. Ask. I've time.

HECUBA: Do you remember, once,
              You came to Troy in disguise,
              A spy? Ragged clothes, filthy,
              Matted blood from eyes to chin?

ODYSSEUS: I remember.

HECUBA: And Helen recognised you?
              Told no one else but me?

ODYSSEUS: A dangerous situation. I remember.

HECUBA: You knelt at my feet -

ODYSSEUS: Clutched hard your dress -

HECUBA: At my mercy.
              Do you remember what you said?

ODYSSEUS: Anything: anything at all,
              To save my skin.

HECUBA: And I spared you - sent you safe away?

ODYSSEUS: I owe you my life.

HECUBA: Then aren't you ashamed
Of these plans of yours?
I treated you... as you say I treated you -
And how do you treat us?
With harm, with harm!
Loathsome you are, you politicians,
Toadies for applause!
You betray your friends
To gratify the mob.
What makes this so clever -
Child-sacrifice, human sacrifice –
Why do they think so?
Have they no cattle to grace this grave?
Achilles came , demanding life for life -
Then why pick her?
What harm has she done him?
Helen:
He could have marked her for sacrifice:
She brought him to Troy,
Brought him to death.
You want to butcher a prisoner.
Fine. Pick her:
Helen of Sparta,
The prettiest, the guiltiest.

So much for justice. As for gratitude -
You knelt to me,
You touched my hand, my cheek,
You begged me. I do the same to you.
Give back to me
The kindness I did you then.
Leave me my child. Don't kill her.
Enough have died.
When I see her I smile, forget my pain;
She's my Troy, my staff,
My guide, my life.
Power brings obligation,

Not to use that power for harm.
And power is fleeting: it flies, it flies.
Once, fortune smiled on me.
No more. One day,
One single day, stole all my happiness.
Odysseus, I kneel to you.
Show mercy, pity.
Go to the Greeks, persuade them.
How can they kill
Women they should have killed before -
Then,
When they dragged them from Troy,
And pitied them?
You've a law in Greece:
Murder is murder,
Be the victim free, or slave.
Tell them, Odysseus.
Your reputation:
You'll persuade them.
Use what words you please,
You'll persuade them.
When a nobody,
And a person of reputation,
Use the same arguments,
Who hears the nobody?

CHORUS: Who is so hard,
           That when they hear these words,
           These cries,
           They will not be moved to tears?

ODYSSEUS: Hecuba, be told.
           You're angry. Don't make enemies
           Of those who give you good advice.
           You saved my life;
           I'm happy to save yours.
           I give my word.
           But I repeat what I said before,

To the Greeks in council.
Troy is taken; Achilles,
Noblest of Greeks,
Demands your daughter's life;
He must have it.
It happens often, too often,
That we honour heroes, warlords,
No more than ordinary men.
Achilles died, for Greece,
As bravely as any man can die.
He's earned our honour. Earned it.
Are we to smile, make friends,
When a man's alive,
And ignore him once he's dead?
Disgraceful!
Imagine another war, another call-up.
Who'd go to fight,
Who'd not sit safe at home, if he saw
How little honour we paid our dead?
Take me: alive, I ask for little,
Just enough. But when I'm dead, I want
An honoured grave, a high-heaped tomb
For all to see. Those honours last.

Unendurable, you say?
I should pity you?
At home in Greece
We've mothers - fathers too -
Weeping; widows
Whose husbands are dust in Troy.
Endure it.
We're Greeks; we honour our dead;
If you blame us for that,
We'll take the blame.
It's your custom here
To stop loving those you love,
To give no respect
To those who died for you? So be it!

Greeks; non-Greeks;
We'll prosper as we deserve.

CHORUS:

Aee, aee.
Slavery. Pain.
We're forced.
We bear what can't be borne.

HECUBA:

Polyxena, child, I begged for your life;
My words were smoke, thin air.
Will he listen to you,
Where your mother failed?
Be a nightingale, sing, sing for dear life.
Down, on your knees.
Make him listen.
He's a father, has children.
Make him listen.

POLYXENA:

Do you flinch, my lord?
Do you turn away?
Don't worry. I won't beg.
I won't embarrass you.
I'll go with you. I'll die. I must.
I want it:
Only a coward would struggle now.
What use is life to me?
My father was king of kings.
That was my life. I was a princess,
Brought up for glittering royal marriage.
Kings fought for my hand,
To make me queen.
Look at me! Once every woman in Troy,
Old, young, looked up to me.
I was a god to them,
Except that gods don't die.
Now I'm a slave. A 'slave'.
I can't bear that. I'd rather die.

Who'll buy me, pay money for me -
A job lot, perhaps,
'Hector's sister and miscellaneous'? -
Some disciplinarian,
Wanting his money's worth,
Who'll put me to bread-making,
Weaving, sweeping floors,
Sharing my bed
With some bought-in male
Who'll paddle and paw
What princes fought for?
No. Die, rather.
Choose to die. Give myself to death.
Take me away, lord.
Do what you have to do.
What else have I left? What future?
No hope, no joy. Don't stop me, mother.
Don't touch. Don't speak.
Accept my death, a noble death, now,
Before they soil us.
We're not used to this.
We could endure the yoke,
But not the shame of it,
Not dishonour.
No. Better die. Better die.

CHORUS: Good breeding gleams like gold
                Among common coins. Miraculous
                When noble spirit matches noble birth.

HECUBA: Fine words, Polyxena.
                But the price is pain. Odysseus,
                Do Achilles the honour he demands,
                Avoid disgrace - but leave the child.
                Take me instead.
                Let my blood drench his grave.
                My son it was who shot the arrow,

Killed him.

ODYSSEUS: Achilles' ghost demanded her, not you.

HECUBA: In that case kill me too, beside her.
Twice as much blood, for Mother Earth,
For Achilles' ghost that asks such things.

ODYSSEUS: It's enough that your daughter dies.
We owe one death. I wish it were none.

HECUBA: I'll die with her. I must.

ODYSSEUS: I give the orders.

HECUBA: I'll cling, as ivy clings to oak.

ODYSSEUS: Take my advice -

HECUBA: I'll not let her go.

ODYSSEUS: I'll not go back without her.

POLYXENA: Hush, mother. Sir, be patient.
She's losing her child. Be patient.
Mother, give way. They're stronger.
They'll knock you down;
They'll drag you, hustle you –
Is that what you want?
An old woman, shamed and bruised -
By boys? No. Accept. Be dignified.
Mother. Darling. Hold me. Kiss me.
I'll never see the Sun again -
So big, so bright.
Only darkness now.
No more words, mother.
Mummy. Goodbye.

HECUBA: For you, child, pity.
               For me, tears, pain.

POLYXENA: I'll be far away,
               In the Underworld, at peace.

HECUBA: Oee, moee.
               What can I do? How can I die?

POLYXENA: A princess - I die a slave.

HECUBA: I live, a slave. I see the Sun, a slave.

POLYXENA: No husband. No marriage.

HECUBA: All my children, gone.

POLYXENA: What shall I tell them, Hector, Priam?

HECUBA: Tell them my misery, my tears.

POLYXENA: Dear breasts that gave me life.

HECUBA: My darling, snatched by fate.

POLYXENA: Farewell.
               Tell Cassandra farewell from me.

HECUBA: Others fare well.
               How shall we fare well?

POLYXENA: And Polydorus, my brother,
               Here in Thrace.

HECUBA: If he's alive. If fate has spared his life.

POLYXENA: He lives. He'll close your eyes in death.

HECUBA: I'm dead. I'm alive, and look: I'm dead.

POLYXENA: Take me, lord. Veil me.
                My tears, my mother's tears.
                Light of day! Your name is all I have.
                You're mine for a little moment more -
                And then Achilles' grave, the knife.

HECUBA: Oee. I'm fainting. Help me.
                Polyxena, hold me. Your hand.
                Child. Don't go. I'm dead.

Exeunt Odysseus and Polyxena. Music.

CHORUS: Winds, winds of the sea,   [*strophe*]
                Swift ships on racing sea,
                Where will you take me, where?
                Who'll own me? Who'll own these tears?
                What harbour, where?
                In the south?
                There on the plains,
                Where Apidanus, father of rivers,
                Makes fertile fields?

                An island home, perhaps?   [*antistrophe*]
                Is Delos to see my tears?
                Delos, where palm and bay
                Spread branches, made holy shade
                When Leto bore
                Apollo,
                Artemis, twins,
                Children of Zeus on high. Shall I dance,
                Dance for them, dance?

                In Athens?   [*strophe*]
                Shall I weave for Athene,
                Bright colours, silk?

What patterns, then?
Mares, yoked to her chariot?
Titans, braving the gods,
Thunder, lightning,
Laid low by Father Zeus?

No children.   [*antistrophe*]
No father now, no country.
Smoke, ruin, slaves.
In a foreign land,
Strangers, they'll call me slave.
Torn from the land I love,
A slave, a slave,
No better than the Dead.

Music ends. Enter Talthybius.

TALTHYBIUS: Trojans, where will I find Hecuba,
                Who once was queen?

CHORUS: There. Face covered.
                Lying on the ground.

TALTHYBIUS: O Zeus! Are there gods?
                Do they see what humans do?
                Or do we believe in vain?
                Blind chance rules all?
                Look, here: the queen of golden Troy,
                King Priam's queen,
                The proud, the prosperous -
                A slave, uncitied, childless,
                Lying on the ground.
                She's nothing. Grey head, dust-crowned.
                Feoo feoo.
                I've lived a long life,
                But still I'd rather die than come to this.
                Poor lady, up. Stand up.

Your grey hairs, up.

HECUBA: Leave me. Let me lie.
               Let me weep.
               Who are you?

TALTHYBIUS: Talthybius, lady.
               High Steward of the Greeks.
               Agamemnon sent me. I've to take you -

HECUBA: To Achilles' grave? To die?
               Oh thank you. Lead the way.

TALTHYBIUS: She's dead, lady. Your daughter, dead.
               I'm fetching you to bury her.
               I speak their will:
               Agamemnon, Menelaus,
               The whole Greek army.

HECUBA: Oee moee.
               Not die? Not fetch me to die?
               To tell me this?
               Polyxena! They snatched you, child,
               They murdered you,
               They took my child.
               How can I bear it?
               Tell me. How did you finish her?
               With respect?
               Or butchering an enemy?
               I'll bear it. Tell me.

TALTHYBIUS: Lady, I wept before,
               When I watched her die.
               Now you ask me to tell it,
               I'll weep again.
               There, gathered at the graveside,
               The whole Greek army,
               To watch the sacrifice.

I was close by.
Achilles' son took Polyxena's hand,
Led her on to the mound, left her.
A detachment of men, hand-picked,
In case the victim struggled. Achilles' son
Took a golden cup, lifted it,
Poured an offering to his father.
Signed to me
To call for silence. Up I stepped.
'Greeks! Be quiet! Be calm! Be still!'
No sound. The whole crowd - still.
He said, 'Achilles, father,
Accept this offering,
Come up from the Underworld.
Dark blood, virgin blood,
Drink it, it's yours,
Our gift to you, from me,
From every Greek.
Smile on us. Watch us, and smile on us,
As we hoist our anchors
And sail for home.
Grant us safe journey. Home!'
He finished.
The army echoed his prayer.
He drew his sword,
The gold inlay. He signed
To the execution party: hold her.
She saw what they intended.
'Greeks' she said,
'You sacked my city.
I die of my own free will.
Don't touch me.
I won't flinch, won't struggle.
Let me die freely,
Go free to the Underworld.
A princess - don't make me a slave
Among the dead. Don't shame me.'
The soldiers heard and cheered.

Lord Agamemnon
Told them to let her go. Then, then,
She took her dress, ripped it
From neck to navel.
She showed her breasts,
Her midriff, beautiful as a statue.
She slipped to her knees.
Achilles' son. She spoke
Her bravest, saddest words of all.
'Choose, prince.
Here, if you will - my heart -
Or here - my throat. I'm ready. Stab.'
He pitied her.
He was reluctant, eager, all at once.
He cut her windpipe. Fountain of blood.
She was dying.
And still she took good care
To fall modestly,
To hide what no man should see.

Her soul left her body.
At once, bustle. The whole army, busy.
Some gather leaves to strew the body.
Some fetch logs, to make a pyre.
Those who stood with empty hands
Were jeered. 'For shame!
Bring gifts. Clothes, ornaments.
She was noble, brave,
A princess, unmatched.'

That's how she died, lady.
No mother on Earth
Could boast a better child,
Or harsher fate.

CHORUS: Pain.
                 See how the gods send pain

On Priam's children,
The land of Troy.

HECUBA: Polyxena, where am I to look?
How am I to weep?
Pain leapfrogs pain.
This latest misery, your death,
How can I not shed tears?
And yet, so royal, so noble -
To die like that - you take away the sting.
It's strange.
Poor soil, if the gods send rain,
Bears fertile crops, belies its nature.
Good soil, deprived of nourishment,
Grows barren.
But human nature never changes.
Bad is bad, good good,
Whatever the blows of fate.
Do we inherit this or learn it?
Good we can teach,
Good upbringing shows that -
And if we know good,
We can use it
As a yardstick to measure bad.

What am I saying?
Talthybius, ask the Greeks,
For me, that no one touch my daughter.
Soldiers, sailors, a mass of men,
Hotter than fire, they lead each other on.
Indiscipline. Keep them away.

(to Attendant:)
And you. Take a basin,
Down to the shore,
Fill it with water.
I'll wash her, the last time,

Spoiled virgin, bride no-bride.
I'll lay her out
As she deserves.
How can I? I've nothing.
I'll ask my fellow-captives,
Here in these tents.
They'll give what they can,
Jewels perhaps,
Snatched up from home,
From looters' hands,
They'll give them for Polyxena.
Troy! Palace! Happiness! Priam,
Most blest of princes, blest of fathers,
And I, most blest of mothers.
Gone. All gone.
We're old. They've robbed us.
Robbed our pride.
Human arrogance!
Pride in possessions! Fame!
We preen like cocks on a dunghill.
It's nothing.
Ambition, eloquence: nothing.
What's happiness?
A life without suffering,
Day by careful day.

Exeunt all but Chorus. Music.

CHORUS: That day began it,   [*strophe*]
                 Began disaster, pain,
                 That day when Paris,
                 High on Mount Ida,
                 Felled trees, built ships,
                 To steal across swelling sea
                 To Helen's bed. Helen!
                 Whose beauty
                 Warmed golden Sun himself.

Now misery, now pain,   [*antistrophe*]
Swarms on us, surrounds us.
One man's madness
Brought common pain,
Destruction for Troy.
He herded sheep on the mountain;
Heard goddesses squabbling;
Judged; began
Common misery, brought pain.

War. Torment. Blood.
In Troy, in Greece.
Over there,
By the banks of sweet Eurotas,
See how she weeps,
Young girl, husbandless,
How grey-haired mothers
Beat their heads,
Tear cheeks,
Blood-nails for slaughtered sons.

> *Music ends. Enter Attendant. Others bring a
> shrouded corpse.*

ATTENDANT: Women, where's Her Majesty?
             Hecuba,
             Of all men, all women, most miserable,
             Hecuba, queen of tears?

CHORUS: What is it? Such cries, such omens.
             Unsleeping pain. What is it?

ATTENDANT: Unsleeping pain - for Hecuba.
             How can I tell the news I bring,
             And smile?

CHORUS: She's heard you. She's coming: there.

Enter Hecuba:

ATTENDANT: Majesty. How can I speak your pain?
               You're alive, you see the Sun,
               But what else is left for you?
               Your city, your husband, children, gone.

HECUBA: Old wounds. You tell us nothing new.
               Polyxena's body:
               Who told you to bring it here?
               The Greeks were to bury her -
               Or so they said.

ATTENDANT: Poor lady, she doesn't know.
               She weeps for Polyxena.
               She hasn't heard.

HECUBA: Oee. What is it? Cassandra dead,
               The mad one? Is it her you bring?

ATTENDANT: She's alive, lady.
               Save your tears for him.
               It's a man we bring.
               I'll uncover his face.
               You never expected this.

HECUBA: Oee moee.
               Polydorus. My son, dead.
               He was safe with that Thracian.
               Fate crushes me. I'm dead.

               Music.

               Polydorus,
               Aee aee, I knew this,
               Weep, oh weep.

Music ends.

ATTENDANT: You knew your son was dead?

HECUBA: I didn't believe it.

Music.

Now I see, I see.
O misery, tears on tears,
Is no day free of pain?

CHORUS: *(spoken)*
Lady, lady, we suffer, we suffer.

HECUBA: Polydorus, child of my misery, child,
Who killed you, who?
Some god, some mortal?

ATTENDANT: *(spoken)*
I don't know, lady.
I found him on the shore.

HECUBA: Drowned, there on the sand,
Or murdered?

ATTENDANT: *(spoken)*
Sea-waves carried him to shore.

HECUBA: Oh moee, aee aee.
I understand. My dream.
Dark vision. Wings.
You were dead, child,
Gone from daylight.

CHORUS: *(spoken)*
Who killed him? Did the dream tell that?

HECUBA: Our ally... friend...
His Majesty of Thrace.
He was to hide Polydorus here,
To keep him safe.

CHORUS: *(spoken)*
Oee moee. And to get the gold, he killed?

HECUBA: Unspeakable! Unholy! Unendurable!
We trusted him. He butchered my son,
He took a sword and hacked my son.
Look here, look here! I spit on him.

       Music ends.

CHORUS: Who else on Earth ever suffered so?
God presses you down.
Shh, friends.
Agamemnon, our master, comes.

       Enter Agamemnon.

AGAMEMNON: Hecuba, why this delay?
You were to bury your daughter.
You sent Talthybius
To ask that no one touch her.
We did as you asked. We left her -
And still you're here. I'm astonished.
Go, quickly.
We've been scrupulous so far,
Under sad circumstances, scrupulous.
Yah. What body's that?
There, by the tent? A Trojan?
Those are Trojan wrappings. Who is it?

HECUBA: Hecuba, what shall I do?
Say nothing, or fall on my knees to him?

AGAMEMNON: Why turn away? Why tears?
Say what's happened. Who is this?

HECUBA: Perhaps he won't listen. To a slave,
An enemy. I couldn't bear it.

AGAMEMNON: What is it? I can't read your mind.
If you want me to know, then tell me.

HECUBA: And perhaps I'm wrong?
Perhaps he'll listen.
Perhaps he'll be kind.

AGAMEMNON: As you choose.
If you'd rather I didn't know,
If you don't want to speak,
I won't force you.

HECUBA: I need him. For their sakes,
For revenge, I need him.
Don't hesitate. Talk to him. Risk it.
Agamemnon, I'm on my knees.
I beg you. Please.

AGAMEMNON: What is it? Are you asking for freedom?
It's granted.

HECUBA: Freedom? Punishment!
For him, for him.
To see him punished,
I'd live a slave forever.

AGAMEMNON: I don't understand.

HECUBA: I ask your help, lord.

AGAMEMNON: For what?

HECUBA: For him. That corpse.

The one I weep for.

AGAMEMNON: I still don't understand.

HECUBA: I carried him in the womb.
               I bore him. My son.

AGAMEMNON: Poor lady. Which son?
               You had many sons.

HECUBA: None of those who died at Troy.

AGAMEMNON: What are you saying? You've other sons?

HECUBA: No longer. This was my other son.

AGAMEMNON: Where exactly was he,
               When Greeks took Troy?

HECUBA: His father had sent him away,
               To save his life.

AGAMEMNON: Just him? No other royal prince?
               Where to?

HECUBA: Here, lord. To Thrace,
               Where we found him dead.

AGAMEMNON: To Polymestor's court, you mean?

HECUBA: He came with gold.
               It brought him death.

AGAMEMNON: How, death? Who killed him? How?

HECUBA: Polymestor.
               His Thracian Majesty. Our friend.

AGAMEMNON: You're telling me: to get the gold - ?

HECUBA: As soon as he heard
               That you Greeks held Troy.

AGAMEMNON: Where did you find him?
               Who brought him here?

HECUBA: On the shore. This woman found him.

AGAMEMNON: Was she there to look for him?
               Or for something else?

HECUBA: Fetching water,
               To wash my daughter's corpse.

AGAMEMNON: So he was killed and thrown into the sea.

HECUBA: Butchered. Flesh hacked. Then thrown.

AGAMEMNON: How can you bear it?

HECUBA: I'm dead, lord. I feel... nothing.

AGAMEMNON: What woman on Earth
               Was ever so misused?

HECUBA: None. I am all Misuse.
               But now, lord, listen.
               I kneel at your feet.
               If you think what I suffer
               Is the will of God, I'll bear it.
               But if not,
               Then help me punish him,
               That friend no-friend
               Who snapped his fingers at the gods,
               And did this deed.

How often we welcomed him,
A favoured guest,
We smiled on that murderer,
Who killed my son
And tossed him to the waves.
We're slaves. We're powerless.
The gods have power.
Law governs them.
And by that Law we live,
We believe in them,
We distinguish right from wrong.
That Law, my lord,
If you scorn it now,
If you leave unpunished
Friends who murder friends,
Who plunder the god's prerogative,
Then justice dies.
What he did was a crime.
Help me punish him.
Take pity on me.
I'm the picture of misery:
Stand back, like a painter,
And drink me in.
I was a queen, I'm now your slave.
Blessed with children once, now cursed.
Old, cityless, friendless, desolate.
Oee moee. Do you turn away?
Won't you listen? Am I wasting words?
What fools we are!
We lavish our time, we learn
All kinds of skills, we practise them -
But that one skill
We should beggar ourselves to learn,
Persuasion, the power
To get what we want, to influence,
We ignore it - why?
What's left? What hope?
My children are dead;

I'm carried off, booty;
My city's smoke.
There's one thing still,
One argument, unexpected, but possible:
The power of Love.
My lord, at your side, in bed,
My daughter sleeps:
Cassandra, Apollo's mouth.
Do they mean anything, my lord,
Those nights of love?
When she kisses you,
Embraces you, my daughter,
Have you gratitude for that?
The joy of dark?
Then listen: this corpse, d'you see it?
My son? Her brother;
Your bedmate's brother.
Do this for him.

One thing more.
If I'd a thousand tongues,
If some craftsman, some god,
Gave tongues to feet, hands, hair,
They'd kneel to you,
They'd cry my cause.
Agamemnon, Majesty,
Light of all Greece, do it.
Do it. Help me.
An old woman; it's nothing; do it.
You're a good man: serve Justice,
As good men should.
See that criminals, everywhere,
Are punished as they deserve.

CHORUS: It happens. Opposites change.
               Necessity forces them.
               Old friends become enemies;
               Old enemies make friends.

AGAMEMNON: Up, Hecuba.
                  Your plight, your son, your words.
                  I'm moved.
                  For the gods' sake, for justice,
                  I say he should be punished,
                  Your friend no friend.
                  But how can it be done?
                  Army discipline:
                  I won't have them say
                  I plotted with you to kill
                  His Majesty of Thrace -
                  For Cassandra's sake.
                  It's serious. They think this man an ally,
                  Your son an enemy. So you love him -
                  Why should that affect them?
                  Think what to do.
                  I'll help, but I won't offend the Greeks.

HECUBA: Feoo.
                  Slaves, lord. All mortals alive are slaves.
                  To money, fate, the people's voice,
                  A city's laws - not one of us
                  Can do exactly as we choose.
                  You're afraid of your soldiers.
                  Army discipline.
                  Well, I give you your freedom.
                  I'll do it. I'll hurt
                  The man who killed my son.
                  Say yes to that,
                  And keep your hands unstained.
                  But if they run to help him,
                  When he faces what he has to face,
                  If trouble starts: hold them.
                  Don't say it's done for me.
                  Agree to that. Leave all the rest to me.

AGAMEMNON: What rest?

What have you in mind? A sword –
Those trembling hands lift sword
To strike him down?
Poison? And will you work alone?
Who'll help?

HECUBA: The women of Troy will help,
               Here in these tents.

AGAMEMNON: Our prisoners-of-war,
               You mean? Our loot?

HECUBA: They'll help me punish him.

AGAMEMNON: How? Women? Overcome a man?

HECUBA: We're many. We're cunning.

AGAMEMNON: You're women.

HECUBA: And was it not women
               Who took Aegyptus' sons?
               Did women not sweep
               All Lemnos clean of men?
               No more argument.
               Grant this woman here safe-conduct.

               (to the Attendant)
               Go to His Thracian Majesty.
               Say to him: 'Hecuba,
               Who once ruled Troy, needs you.
               Important matters, vital to you both.
               Come with your sons.
               They must hear as well.'
               Agamemnon, my daughter's funeral.
               Make more delay.
               I want them together, my two darlings,

Brother and sister. One pyre. One grave.

AGAMEMNON: It's granted.
             If the wind had been fair for Greece
             I'd have refused.
             But the gods send storms.
             We have to wait. Patience.
             God send good luck -
             It's understood, for states,
             For private individuals,
             That the good should prosper,
             The wicked fail.

> *Exeunt Agamemnon and Attendant. The body is
> removed. Music.*

CHORUS: Troy! Home!   [*strophe*]
             My Troy, destroyed.
             A cloud of Greeks,
             A storm of spears.
             Stolen, your crown of towers,
             Fire-stormed. I weep for you.
             I leave you. Weep and leave.

             Night. Death.   [*antistrophe*]
             Sleep charmed my eyes.
             Supper, singing,
             Dancing, all done,
             A feast of joy. They'd gone!
             Greeks, gone! Men, ships, all gone.
             My husband rested, slept.

             I was putting up my hair,   [*strophe*]
             For bed, for sleep, under its cap;
             Gold mirror gleamed.
             Soft bed. Blankets.
             Outside, a shout:
             'Men of Greece, it's now.

Sack Troy, the towers of Troy,
Sail home!'

I left the marriage-bed   [*antistrophe*]
I loved. In a shift I sat,
Like some Greek girl,
Suppliant. The temple.
They murdered my husband,
Shipped me away.
I looked back at my Troy,
And wept.

I cursed her then,
Helen of Sparta,
Hell to Troy;
Cursed Paris,
Her mate, our fate.
They came together,
Made a marriage,
No marriage,
Made a household,
Uprooted me from mine.
Death they were;
Plague they were.
Helen! Drown!
Come never home!

> *Music ends. Enter Polymestor and his Sons,
> attended.*

POLYMESTOR: O Priam, dearest of men. O Hecuba,
Your city gone, your daughter dead,
I weep for you. Feoo.
Nothing lasts. Fame? Rank? They pass.
God blurs our lives, jumbles them -
We see no pattern; we worship God.
But these are empty tears. No help.
Hecuba, I should have been here before.

Don't blame me.
When they brought you to Thrace
I was far away, up-country.
As soon as I came home,
I was setting out to see you,
Foot out of the door,
When she arrived, your servant.
She spoke; I'm here.

HECUBA: Polymestor, I can't look you in the face.
I'm ashamed. I flounder in misery.
You knew me before; you see me now;
I can't look at you. Don't blame me.
Not just you, Polymestor. Any man.
From men, women veil their eyes.

POLYMESTOR: Quite right. But you sent for me.
'Come at once,' you said. What is it?

HECUBA: Something private,
For your ears only,
Yours and your sons'.
Have the guards withdraw.

POLYMESTOR: *(to Guards)*
Leave us. We're safe.
There's no one here.

(to Hecuba, as they go)
No quarrel with the Greeks,
And none with you.
Now, tell me. If a man's blessed by fate
He should help unluckier friends.
I'm yours.

HECUBA: First, tell me: my son, Polydorus,
The child I sent you, his father sent you.

Is he alive? No other question first.

POLYMESTOR: He's fine. Don't worry.

HECUBA: You speak like the friend you are.

POLYMESTOR: What other questions? Ask.

HECUBA: Does he speak of me? Remember me?

POLYMESTOR: He wants to come to you, here, in secret.

HECUBA: And the gold he brought from Troy?
              It's safe?

POLYMESTOR: Safe in my palace. Guarded.

HECUBA: Look after it. Beware of greed.

POLYMESTOR: My dear, I have what I have.
              I'm satisfied.

HECUBA: So. What I have to say,
              To you and your sons -

POLYMESTOR: I'm waiting to hear.

HECUBA: It's a secret.
              You're such a trusted friend -

POLYMESTOR: You can tell us: myself, my sons.

HECUBA: Ancestral gold. Priam's. Hidden.

POLYMESTOR: I'm to tell your son?

HECUBA: Who else can I trust?

POLYMESTOR: These children. Do they need to hear?

HECUBA: In case you die. They'd need to know.

POLYMESTOR: I hadn't thought of that.

HECUBA: In Troy, where Athene's temple stood -

POLYMESTOR: It's there, the gold? Is there a marker?

HECUBA: A black rock jutting from the ground.

POLYMESTOR: I'll remember. Something else?

HECUBA: I want you to have the things I brought.

POLYMESTOR: What things?
                Are you carrying them? Inside?

HECUBA: Inside, with all the other plunder. Safe.

POLYMESTOR: Safe? Here?
                The Greek ships' loading-point?

HECUBA: The tents of the female prisoners
                Are out of bounds.

POLYMESTOR: And safe? No guards inside? No men?

HECUBA: No Greeks. Just women. Just us.
                Come inside. The Greeks are panting
                To sail. They long for home.
                As soon as you've got what's yours,
                You and the boys,
                You can go where you left my son.

                Exeunt all but Chorus. Music.

CHORUS: It's coming, soon. You'll pay.
You're in the rapids,
You're drowning,
Swept from your heart's desire
Because of the life you stole.
There's a debt to pay,
To the gods, to Justice,
And the price is pain, is pain.
You're lost, on the road to Hell.
No warrior's hand will cut you down.

POLYMESTOR: *(inside)*
Omoee!
Help me! They're blinding me.

CHORUS: Ladies, was that His Majesty?
Such shrieks!

POLYMESTOR: *(inside)*
Omoee, moee!
The children! Blood.

CHORUS: Ladies, inside:
Unspeakable, unheard-of.

POLYMESTOR: *(inside)*
Run, run, you won't escape.
I'll tear every corner,
I'll smash, I'll smash.

CHORUS: Should we go in? Is this the time?
Hecuba, her women -
Do they need us now?

Enter Hecuba. Music ends.

HECUBA: Tear! Smash! Splinter the doors!
You won't smash back your sight,

> Won't splinter back your sons,
> Won't see them alive again.
> I killed them.

CHORUS:

> Majesty! It's done?
> You've tripped him, the Thracian?
> You've done it? You've done it?

HECUBA:

> See for yourself. He's coming.
> Blind, stumbling. You'll see his sons.
> We killed them. My women; I. He's paid.
> He's here. Thracian fury. Raging.
> I'll stand aside.

Enter Polymestor, blind. Music.

POLYMESTOR:

> O moee, eYOH,
> Paee BOH, paee STOH, paee kelSOH.
> Where am I to go? What rest? What lair?
> Four legs, a beast, crawling?
> I sniff them out, here, or here,
> Murderers, Trojans, women.
> I'm dead.
> They killed me, Trojans, women.
> Die! Die!
> Where are you hiding? Where?
> Help me, my eyes, light of the Sun,
> O give me back my eyes.
>
> A! A!
> Something's moving.
> Women. I'll jump on them,
> I'll munch them, flesh, bones,
> I'll feast on them, they'll pay.
> They hurt me. Pay.
>
> Where shall I go?

Shall I leave my sons?
To be butchered, torn,
Dog-meat. Where are they?
I'm a ship, skimming the sea,
Sail billowing, beached, furled,
Here in the lair of death
To save my sons.

CHORUS: *(spoken)*
                 Poor wretch. They've hurt you so.
                 You killed; they've punished you.
                 Gods' work.

POLYMESTOR: Aee aee, eeoh,
                 Men of Thrace!
                 Bring spears, shields, horses.
                 Eeoh Greeks,
                 Eeoh Agamemnon, Menelaus!
                 BoAHN, boAHN, aeeTOH boAHN!
                 In gods' name, help me.
                 Now. I'm begging. Help.
                 They've killed me,
                 Your women, your booty,
                 They've spoiled me.
                 Omoee. For shame.
                 Where go? Where turn?
                 Up, up, sky-vault, dazzle, burning eyes,
                 Or down, dark water, the deeps of Hell?

CHORUS: *(spoken)*
                 To suffer so! How can he bear it?
                 If he cast loose from his life,
                 Who'd blame him now?

                 Music ends. Enter Agamemnon, attended.

AGAMEMNON: Howling. Yelling. I came at once.

Echo ran from the hills,
Ran through the camp, uproar.
If we'd not known Troy was ours,
Its towers rubble,
There might have been panic.

POLYMESTOR: Agamemnon. Your voice.
My dear. D'you see?
D'you see what they've done to me?

AGAMEMNON: Eah.
Polymestor.
What's happened? Who hurt you?
Your eyes, the blood. Your sons,
Dead. Who killed them.
Whose rage is this we see?

POLYMESTOR: Hecuba. Her women.
They hurt me. They did.

AGAMEMNON: I don't believe it. Hecuba?
What he said?
What made you do
Such a terrible thing?

POLYMESTOR: Omoee. She's here. Somewhere.
Show me. I'll tear her. I'll crimson her.

AGAMEMNON: Be still.

POLYMESTOR: I want her, give her, in the name of God.
These hands. I want her. Here.

AGAMEMNON: Control yourself. You're like a wild animal.
Speak sensibly, calmly. I'll hear you.
Your suffering, what caused it.
Then she can speak.
I'll hear; I'll judge.

POLYMESTOR: Listen. There was a child: Polydorus,
Their youngest son, hers and Priam's.
Priam sent him from Troy to me,
Suspected that Troy would fall,
Sent him to me for safety.
I killed him. I'll tell you why -
Good reasons, common sense.
If he lived, your enemy,
If he survived, he'd gather Troy,
Rebuild it; you Greeks would hear
That one of Priam's sons still lived;
You'd make another expedition,
Land here in Thrace,
Plunder. Disaster for Troy's neighbours.
We had it before. Agamemnon... ?

She heard he was dead. She sent for me.
Some tale of gold,
Priam's gold, a hoard of it in Troy.
No one else was to know.
She took me in there. My sons.
I sat on a couch. Lay back.
The women beside me.
This side, that side.
Conversation, politeness.
'Such wonderful weave, your cloak.
May we see it against the light?
And these are Thracian spears?'
So they stripped me of both. Unarmed.
Others picked up my sons,
Dandled them,
Passed them to one another -
Away from their father.
Then, suddenly, politeness ends.
Daggers -
Where from? Their clothes?
They stab the boys.
I'm held. Arms, legs.

They grip like an octopus.
I try to get up, to help the children.
They grab my hair.
My arms, gripped to my sides.
Outnumbered.
Then - horrible, horrible - they take pins,
Brooches, stab my eyes, blood, pulp.
They hide. They run away.
I'm a wild beast, springing,
Scrabbling after them,
Wild dogs, a hunter,
Battering, smashing.

That's what they did. I helped you,
Agamemnon,
I killed your enemy -
And that's what they did to me.
I've one thing more to say.
Whatever names men find
For women, now, in the past,
In future time,
Come down to this: they're monsters,
Unheard-of, unique on land,
On sea. Who sees them, knows it.

CHORUS: Outrageous!
               You're hurt, you lash out,
               You condemn all women equally.
               Outrageous!

HECUBA: Agamemnon,
               What people say and what they do!
               If only goodness shone
               In all good people said,
               If only criminals betrayed themselves,
               Instead of using words
               To twist their wickedness to good -

It's a skill, you can learn it,
But it doesn't last.
In the end you trip yourself,
No one avoids it,
You trip and fall.

So be it. I'll answer him.
You say you killed my son
To save the Greeks
A second expedition -
For Agamemnon's sake.
You're lying.
In the first place, how could you,
Barbarians,
Ever see eye to eye with Greeks?
Oil and water. Impossible.
Something else
Made you so eager, so hot for them.
Did you want - you can't have wanted -
Some kind of royal marriage?
Was it really to save your crops
Being trampled, if they came again?
Are we to believe such lies?
It was gold, greed for gold,
That killed my son.
If you'd wanted to gratify the Greeks,
This man, you could have taken
The child you were rearing
And killed him years ago,
While Troy still stood,
While Priam still ruled,
While Hector lived.
You could have delivered
My son to them alive.
Instead you waited,
And when the city fell,
When fires blazed its end,

You took him then,
An ally, a guest in your house,
And murdered him.

A second betrayal.
You say you love the Greeks.
And yet, when they were desperate,
Far from home, in want,
Did you take the gold –
His gold, you admit it – and give it them?
You hugged it for your own.
Locks, strongrooms, you hug it still.
If you'd kept my son as you should,
Looked after him,
The whole world would have praised you
As a loyal friend – not in good times,
When friends are cheap, but in bad
When true friendship shows itself.
If you'd been poor,
And my son had been safe,
He'd have brought you more than gold.
As it is, you've nothing: no ally,
No hope in the gold, no sons, no eyes.

Agamemnon, if you help this traitor,
Liar, thief, false friend,
You'll share his vileness.
Pitch, my lord –
I say it respectfully, slave to lord –
Pitch sticks.

CHORUS: Feoo feoo.
True cause, true words.
It's always so.

AGAMEMNON: This... vileness you speak of
Is nothing to do with me. I'm not involved.
It weighs on me, to settle it.

But I agreed. I'll do it. My view is this:
You killed a guest not for my sake,
Not for the Greeks, but for gold,
To keep his gold. Now you're trapped,
You wriggle. Fair-seeming lies.
You people here may think
It's nothing to murder guests.
In Greece, it's a crime.
If I declare you innocent,
I condemn myself.
You did it; you didn't flinch;
Don't cower now you're caught.

Music.

POLYMESTOR: Oee moee. She's a woman, a slave –
Am I to submit to this?

HECUBA: You killed; it's just; you suffer.

POLYMESTOR: Oee moee. My sons. My eyes.

HECUBA: Tears for your child?
Like mine, for mine?

POLYMESTOR: Murderer. You smile?

HECUBA: Avenger. I smile.

POLYMESTOR: Not for long. The sea –

HECUBA: Will float me away to Greece?

POLYMESTOR: Will drown you.
From the mast you'll fall.

HECUBA: They'll make me walk the mast?
[*alternative:* From the mast? They'll

make me jump?]

POLYMESTOR: You'll climb there.

HECUBA: Will I have wings, or what?

POLYMESTOR: A dog you'll be. Hyena. Crimson eyes.

HECUBA: I'm to change my shape? Who told you?

POLYMESTOR: Our oracle here in Thrace -

HECUBA: Told you that?
               And nothing about yourself?

POLYMESTOR: If it had, d'you think
               You'd have tricked me so?

HECUBA: And when I've changed,
               Am I to die, or live?

POLYMESTOR: You'll die. Your monument -

HECUBA: Called after my new, changed shape?

POLYMESTOR: 'Bitch Grave' - a landmark for sailors.

HECUBA: I'll bear it. I've made you pay.

POLYMESTOR: And - Cassandra, your daughter.
               She must die.

HECUBA: Spit on you. You die.

POLYMESTOR: His wife will murder her.
               The Fury waits.

HECUBA: His wife? God turn away such madness.

POLYMESTOR: She'll kill him too. She'll lift the axe -

AGAMEMNON: That's enough. Are you mad?
               D'you want more pain?

POLYMESTOR: Oh, kill me. In Argos,
               You'll bathe in blood.

AGAMEMNON: Take him. No mercy.

POLYMESTOR: You can't bear to hear?

AGAMEMNON: Gag him.

POLYMESTOR: Too late. It's said.

               Music ends.

AGAMEMNON: Find a desert island. Maroon him.
               Such insolence!
               Hecuba, lady, go now.
               Bury your children.
               Women, hurry to your owners' tents.
               The wind's rising, to speed us home.
               God grant us safe voyage,
               A happy homecoming,
               After so much turmoil here.

               Music.

CHORUS: Go to the tents, the ships. My dears.
               Learn your new duties, your slavery.
               It's fate; it's hard.

               Exeunt.

HELEN

This translation was commissioned by the Gate Theatre and was given a rehearsed reading there on March 26th, 1995, directed by Gaynor MacFarlane, as part of a Euripides season centred on the three plays produced as *Agamemnon's Children*.

CHARACTERS

HELEN
TEUCER
MENELAUS
*DOORKEEPER
SAILOR
THEONOE
THEOCLYMENUS
SERVANT
CASTOR

POLLUX, GUARDS, ATTENDANTS (silent parts)

CHORUS OF GREEK WOMEN PRISONERS

*in the original: 'Old Woman'

Before the royal palace in Egypt. To one side, a pyramid. Enter Helen.

HELEN: We're in Egypt. Flat fields,
                         Watered by melted snow, not rain,
                         White snow from the mountains:
                         The lovely Nile. The Old Man of the Sea
                         Ruled here in mortal form.
                         He lived on a little island, Pharos,
                         So he called himself Pharaoh.
                         Egypt's king.
                         He married a sea-nymph:
                         Psammathe, 'Sandy';
                         They had two children, a boy
                         (Theoclymenus), and a girl
                         Called Pretty when she was a baby,
                         And when she was older Theonoe,
                         'Knows about the gods'. Her Reverence -
                         She's a prophetess, tells past and future,
                         As her grandfather did before her,
                         The Old Man of the Sea's old father.

                         I'm not Egyptian.
                         You'll have heard of me.
                         Tyndareus' daughter, from Sparta -
                         Or possibly not Tyndareus' daughter.
                         There's a story that Zeus
                         Turned into a swan,
                         Pretended to be chased
                         By an eagle, fluttered for shelter
                         Into the lap of Leda my mother -
                         You can guess the rest. It may be true.
                         Helen, my name is. Ill-used Helen.
                         I'll explain.
                         There was a beauty contest,
                         On Mount Ida
                         Not far from Troy. The judge was Paris,
                         Prince Paris, the contestants

Were three goddesses,
Hera, Athene, Aphrodite. The last one,
Our Lady of Desire, used bribes to win.
She offered Paris me:
If he let her win he could marry me,
The most beautiful woman
In all the world.
(People are always telling me,
'How lucky you are, to be so beautiful'.)
He let her win.
He left his flocks and herds
On Mount Ida
And came to Sparta to get me.

Unfortunately, since Aphrodite won,
The others lost.
Hera was not pleased.
She spoiled it for Paris.
He thought he was getting
Helen of Sparta,
But in fact she took a cloud,
Made an image, exactly like me,
Breathed life into it, gave it to him,
He thought it was me, it wasn't.
Then Zeus took a hand, stirred up war
Between Greece and Troy. Two reasons:
To cull the human race
(His private reason);
To discover the greatest hero in Greece
(His official reason).
It wasn't my fault. The Greeks
Said they were fighting Troy for me,
But I wasn't even there.
Hermes gathered me up,
Parceled me in cloud
And dumped me here
In Egypt, in Pharaoh's palace.
They trusted him,

The Old Man of the Sea, I mean,
To keep me safe for Menelaus
While the war was on.
So, I'm an evacuee,
My husband is toppling Troy
To fetch me,
Thousands are dying for me,
Beside that Trojan river, Scamander.
The Greeks hate me.
'Helen Hell to men',
They call me. I started it, they say,
It was all my fault. It wasn't.

So what am I supposed to do?
Kill myself? I can't. A prophecy.
When Hermes dumped me here,
He said that one day I'd be back
In Sparta,
Ruling with Menelaus in Sparta.
They'd tell him
(Menelaus) that I didn't go to Troy,
Didn't go to bed with... anyone.
Well, not so far.
It was fine while the Old Man
Was Pharaoh.
But now he isn't, now he's left the Earth,
The son's succeeded - and he wants me,
Keeps after me. What can I do?
I stay out here,
By the Old Man's pyramid.
It's a holy place,
Sanctuary, they can't touch me here.
I may not be popular in Greece,
But at least I'm pure.

Enter Teucer.

TEUCER: Good God, what a place. Just look at it!

Who on Earth rules a pile like this?

He sees Helen.

Ea.
It's her! Helen Hell to men,
Who toppled Troy, who ruined Greece -
Or someone very like her. I'm sorry:
The gods really must hate you,
To give you that face... It's incredible...
If I hadn't been a stranger here,
One arrow,
One well-aimed arrow, would've...

HELEN: How dare you?
                I don't know who you are,
                But whatever she did,
                You can't blame me.

TEUCER: I'm sorry. I shouldn't have...
                But you are amazingly...
                Helen Hell to men...
                I'm terribly sorry.

HELEN: And your name? Nationality?

TEUCER: Greek. Alas.

HELEN: No wonder you don't like Helen.
                You do have a name?

TEUCER: Teucer. Prince of Salamis.
                Son of King Telamon.

HELEN: Then you're well off course.
                This is Egypt.

TEUCER: They banished me.

HELEN: Oh, bad luck. Who?

TEUCER: My father: imagine.

HELEN: It does seem hard. What for?

TEUCER: My brother Ajax died at Troy.

HELEN: Fighting bravely with spear and sword?

TEUCER: Suicide, actually.

HELEN: Mad, was he?

TEUCER: You've heard the name... Achilles?

HELEN: Wasn't he one of Helen's suitors,
            Years ago?

TEUCER: He died,
            And his armour caused big trouble.

HELEN: For your brother?

TEUCER: They gave it to someone else,
            So he killed himself.

HELEN: But how does that...?
            I mean, why do you...?

TEUCER: Simple: he died, I survived. That's all.

HELEN: You fought at Troy?

TEUCER: To the end. I wish it had been my end.

HELEN: Troy's gone?

TEUCER: Razed to the ground. Ploughed under.

HELEN: Helen, Hell to Troy.

TEUCER: And Greece.
Don't forget Hell to Greece.

HELEN: How long ago was this?

TEUCER: Seven years.

HELEN: And how long were you all there,
At Troy?

TEUCER: Give or take: ten years.

HELEN: You got her back, that woman?

TEUCER: Menelaus grabbed her hair, and got her.

HELEN: Did you see him do it?
Or did someone tell you?

TEUCER: I saw it, as I see you now.

HELEN: It might have been a trick. The gods...

TEUCER: Don't be silly.

HELEN: You really saw Helen.

TEUCER: I'm a soldier. Trained observer...

HELEN: So she's home with Menelaus, now?
TEUCER: Not a bit of it.

HELEN:	Aee aee. What's happened?
TEUCER:	The pair of them have vanished.
HELEN:	You didn't all sail home together?
TEUCER:	Storms, lady. We were scattered.
HELEN:	Where?
TEUCER:	All over the Aegean.
HELEN:	And no one's seen them since?
TEUCER:	No. Posted missing. Dead.
HELEN:	Then I... What about her mother, Leda?
TEUCER:	Dead. Long ago.
HELEN:	Because of Helen?
TEUCER:	She hanged herself.
HELEN:	Her sons, then? Castor, Pollux? They're not dead as well?
TEUCER:	Dead; not dead. Two versions.
HELEN:	Pardon? *(aside)* This is ridiculous.
TEUCER:	In one, they changed into stars.
HELEN:	And in the other?
TEUCER:	They killed themselves. Her brothers. Let's change the subject. I hate all this.

I'll tell you why I'm here. Theonoe,
I want to see Theonoe the prophetess.
Help me. Translate for me.
I want to know
The best route from here,
In a fast sailing ship,
To Cyprus. It's an island, Apollo said,
And I'm to settle there, found a city.
I'm going to call it Salamis,
After the other one.

HELEN: Don't wait, sail now. Any way you can.
If you stay here, you're dead.
If His Majesty sees you.
He's out, hunting,
But when he comes back...
He hates all Greeks,
Slaughters them. Don't ask me why,
I'm not allowed to tell you. Really.

TEUCER: Thanks, lady. Gods smile on you.
You really do look like her,
Until you speak.
Completely different character.
God drown her,
God keep her from home.
But you, lady: happiness.

Exit. Music.

HELEN: Tears, waves of tears,
How shall I weep? Aee aee.

Sirens, sing with me,   [*strophe*]
Weep with me,
Sirens, Earth's daughters, come,
Flutes, pan-pipes,

Sing with me, weep with me.
Tears from Persephone, queen of Hell,
Bring to me, sing to me,
I'll send her my tears,
My songs,
For Dead below the earth, my songs.

Enter Chorus.

CHORUS: There on sandy shore,   [*antistrophe*]
Dunes, reeds, sea,
Sun bleeding, red-bleeding,
I was there,
Clothes washing, drying, Sun.
I heard her, my lady, tears, bitter tears,
As lonely in the hills
Nymphs sing their ills,
Raped, secret caves,
Pan rapes them, rape.

HELEN: Eeoh eeoh.   [*strophe*]
Friends, Greeks, stolen,
A man came, Greek, he came,
Grief-bringer, tear-bringer.
Troy's gone, its towers,
Troy, for Helen gone.
Leda my mother, hanged,
For Helen shamed.
Menelaus, drowned,
Dark sea, drowned.
My brothers, Castor, Pollux, gone.
Vanished. Their running-place,
There by the banks of Eurotas,
Horses galloping,
All gone.

CHORUS: Aee aee.   [*antistrophe*]

Tears, lady, tears,
A life of tears, of pain.
We weep for you, weep for you.
Zeus, wings, swan-wings,
Beating, for what? For this:
Leda your mother, gone,
Your brothers, gone,
Star-children, gone.
Here you live,
Exiled, here, you sleep in foreign beds,
Your husband drowned. What hope
There by the banks of Eurotas,
What hope of home, going home?
All gone.

HELEN: Feoo feoo.
High in the hills of Troy
Pines fell, pines bled for Troy.
Pine ship, his ship,
That pirate ship sailing, sailing
To steal me from Sparta.
Her fault, Aphrodite's fault,
Desire, death in desire, for Greece.
Flowers, handfuls of flowers,
I was picking flowers,
Flowers for Athene,
When Hermes came, God's messenger,
Hera's messenger,
Picked me, flower of Sparta,
Brought me here to this lonely land,
Brought death to Greece, to Troy.
What did they call me,
There by the streams of Troy?
Whore-Helen! Bitch-Helen! Lies.

Music ends.

CHORUS: It's hard. But bear it.

What else can you do? You must.

HELEN: Friends, I'm an animal, yoked.
I drag my fate along.
Hatched from an egg,
A yolk-sack: who else in all the world
Was born as I was born?
My life's a myth,
A warning. I'm beautiful,
I offended Hera,
What else is to blame?
If I'd been a picture,
They could have rubbed me out,
Started again, ordinary not pretty.
Unknown. Happy.

Some people want just one thing in life,
All their lives, and the gods refuse it.
Hard, but bearable. I suffer,
And suffer, and suffer.
First, and worst,
I've done nothing wrong,
And I'm a criminal.
They lifted me from Greece, the gods,
And dumped me here:
A princess, a slave.
They're all slaves here,
Only Pharaoh's free.
And now my last hope's gone, my anchor
In all this pain,
That he would come, Menelaus,
That he'd take me home -
He's dead, he's gone.

I killed my own mother. I did nothing,
And she died. My daughter, my darling,
Hope of my heart: no husband,
A grey old maid.

My brothers, Castor, Pollux, gone.
A living death: I've nothing.
If I ever went home, who'd welcome me?
Helen, bitch-Helen, they'd say,
Who ran to Troy. I don't exist.
Menelaus might recognise me,
Might be persuaded, know who I was,
But Menelaus is dead. I don't exist.

What alternatives? An Egyptian husband,
Sit at a stranger's table, feast,
A man I despise?
Am I to hate myself? It comes to this:
All women long for loveliness,
I've got it, I'm dead of it.

CHORUS: Helen, you can't tell.
The man who came:
He could have been wrong.

HELEN: Menelaus is dead. He said so, plainly.

CHORUS: People make mistakes.

HELEN: Not always.

CHORUS: You believe the worst, you force yourself.

HELEN: I'm afraid. What else should I be?

CHORUS: Don't they treat you well, inside?

HELEN: All except one. He... pants for me.

CHORUS: Do this, then. Don't stay here -

HELEN: Leave sanctuary?

CHORUS: Go to the prophetess. Her Reverence.
                The sea nymph's daughter. Ask her:
                Is Menelaus alive, does he see the Sun?
                Then weep, or smile, with reason.
                You're tearing yourself for nothing.
                Do it. Leave sanctuary, talk to her -
                A fountain of truth, here in the house,
                Why go elsewhere? We'll help,
                Go in with you, ask with you.
                Women help each other. It's what we do.

                Music.

HELEN: I'll do it. Friends,
                Come in with me,
                Find out with me.

CHORUS: We'll help.

HELEN: Eeoh. Pain, tears,
                What will she tell?

CHORUS: You'll know soon enough.
                No tears. Be calm.

HELEN: Menelaus, my darling -
                Does he see the Sun
                Still soaring, sky-galloping,
                Or is he dead among the dead,
                Eternal dark?

CHORUS: You'll know soon enough.
                Hope now. Please hope.

HELEN: In Sparta, green fields, reeds,
                Wide river: by them I swear,
                If the stranger told true

(And why should he lie?),
If my husband's dead, I'll die -
A noose, a knife, sharp knife
For them, three goddesses,
For Paris, cowherd, die.

CHORUS: God turn this aside,
                 Send happiness.

HELEN: Troy died for nothing.
                 Aphrodite's gifts: beauty,
                 My beauty, for others death,
                 Tears, blood, pain on pain.
                 Mothers wept for sons,
                 For lovers girls chopped their hair,
                 Greece tore soft cheeks,
                 Wept tears of blood.

                 In Arcadia once, they say,
                 Zeus and Callisto once...
                 He changed her, they say,
                 Made her a bear, their child a bear,
                 Soft fur, gentle eyes, no pain
                 Like hers, like Leda's, my mother's -
                 And that other one, he chased her,
                 God made her a deer, golden horns,
                 Took pain away, left loveliness.
                 My loveliness killed Troy,
                 Smashed Troy, tore Greece apart.

                 Music ends. Exeunt. Enter Menelaus, in rags.

MENELAUS: Years ago, Pelops and Oenomaus
                 Raced chariots: I wish they hadn't.
                 Years before that,
                 Pelops' father served him up
                 In a stew for gods,
                 And they refused to eat him.

I wish they had:
He'd never have lived to father my father,
Atreus, who married my mother, Aerope,
Fathered my brother Agamemnon,
And me, Menelaus.
Agamemnon and Menelaus -
What a pair we were. Not to boast,
But we did gather a thousand ships
To topple Troy, the heroes of Greece,
And we did lead by consent, not force.
I remember all their names: some died,
Some sailed safely home, brought news
Of their comrades who died in Troy.
And me?
I left the rubble of Troy, I put to sea,
Grey waves, I wandered, storms,
More storms...
All I wanted was Sparta.
The gods denied me.
Home. Every time I see the hills of home
They snatch me away, the gods,
Send storms to buffet me away.
All I want is home,
All I pray for - and I think I've sailed
To every god-forsaken place in Africa.

Where's this, for example? A rocky coast,
Shipwreck, pieces of ship all round me.
I found a big piece, part of the keel,
Held on, brought to land.
And her, of course, Helen,
She was with me,
The one I brought from Troy.
Where is this place? Who lives here?
I haven't liked to ask,
Haven't wanted to be seen:
A prince in rags,
Down on his luck,

Not like ordinary beggars.
But you have to do it.
Food, we need, clothes -
I mean, look what I'm wearing,
All my royal robes
Went down when the ship...
I put Helen in a cave,
Told her to wait for me,
The one who began all this,
Left the survivors in charge,
And came on here, alone, foraging...

This is some kind of palace,
Vast stones, enormous gates,
Some rich person's home. They'll help.
Always find a rich person's house -
Poor people may want to help,
But what have they got?
A shipwrecked sailor...

Hey! Open up! Who's in charge?
Doorkeeper! A visitor,
Someone needing help.

Enter Doorkeeper.

DOORKEEPER: Who is it? Go away.
                Don't stand there making trouble.
                If you're Greek, you're dead.

MENELAUS: Hey, hey, hey. I just want to talk.
                I just want to talk, and then I'll go.

DOORKEEPER: Go now. 'Don't let anyone in,' they said.
                'No one's to come in. Especially Greeks.'

MENELAUS: Stop pushing.

DOORKEEPER:	I will if you go.
MENELAUS:	Go and tell your master -
DOORKEEPER:	A message from you? I'll smart for it.
MENELAUS:	I'm a prince. Shipwrecked, but princely.
DOORKEEPER:	You've come to the wrong palace.
MENELAUS:	I insist on coming in.
DOORKEEPER:	Oh no you don't.
MENELAUS:	Aee aee. My armies, where are they now?
DOORKEEPER:	You may be big at home. Here, you're small.
MENELAUS:	Oh Gods.
DOORKEEPER:	Tears, now? What's wrong with you?
MENELAUS:	Everything.
DOORKEEPER:	Oh, go back home, cry there.
MENELAUS:	First, please: where is this place?
DOORKEEPER:	Pharaoh's palace.
MENELAUS:	Oh God, not Egypt.
DOORKEEPER:	What's wrong with it?
MENELAUS:	Nothing. What use is it to me?

DOORKEEPER: You're not the only one
                Down on his luck.

MENELAUS: Look, is he in, your master?

DOORKEEPER: The old one's dead. That's his pyramid.
                There's a new one now.

MENELAUS: And is he in or out?

DOORKEEPER: Out. And he can't stand Greeks.

MENELAUS: What have we done? It's not my fault.

DOORKEEPER: You haven't done anything.
                She's here. Helen.

MENELAUS: Pardon?

DOORKEEPER: Zeus' daughter.
                Queen of Sparta. Helen.

MENELAUS: What d'you mean?

DOORKEEPER: She arrived from Sparta.

MENELAUS: I left her in a cave...

DOORKEEPER: No, no, no: before you all went to Troy.
                Go away. It's a bad moment, inside.
                If he catches you here, you're dead.
                I'm sorry: Greeks don't bother me,
                It's the master. I have to talk like this.

                          Exit.

MENELAUS: Now what?
                'A bad moment'? What's that mean?

Worse than before?
I come all the way from Troy,
I leave my wife in a cave, come here -
And there's an impostor in the palace?
Zeus' child, she said.
Is there another Zeus,
Some Egyptian, here in Egypt?
Of course not.
There's only one, lives in the sky.
Another Sparta? Another Troy?
There can't be.
The world's a big place,
Lots of people, lots of cities
Have the same names as each other.
Women, too. Don't be so surprised.
And don't be afraid of her,
She's just a doorkeeper. He'll take me in,
This Pharaoh, her master.
Hear my name, take me in:
I'm not unknown. I toppled Troy.
I'll wait for him here. Two choices:
If he's uncivilised,
I hide, slip back to the wreck;
If he isn't, I make myself known,
Explain what's happened,
Ask for what I need.
How are the mighty fallen! A king
Asking other kings for handouts!
Well, no option.
It's fate, it's hard, as someone said.

Music. Enter Chorus.

CHORUS: Inside, we saw
               Her Reverence,
               The prophetess.
               She answered everything.
               Menelaus isn't dead,

He sees the Sun,
Wild sea he wanders,
Far from home,
A beggar,
Companions dead, bending
His back, his back,
As he rows from Troy.

Enter Helen.

HELEN: Back to sanctuary. She spoke,
Words of hope. She never lies.
He's alive, my husband, he sees the Sun,
A wanderer, sails seven seas,
Exhausted, soon it'll end, in Egypt.
How, end? Alive or dead? She didn't say,
I didn't ask, too happy to hear he's safe.
She said he was here, somewhere here,
Shipwrecked, most companions dead -
Oh moee,
Come, darling, come, please come.

She sees Menelaus.

Ea! Who is it? One of Pharaoh's men?
It's a trap. The tomb, run for the tomb,
Sanctuary, run like a dog, sanctuary...
Look at him. Wild-eyed. He's after me.

MENELAUS: Don't run.
The pyramid, the holy ground,
Don't run. Don't be afraid.
I was amazed when I saw you.
That's all: amazed.

HELEN: Help, women. He won't let me pass.
He's blocking my way. Pharaoh's man.

Kidnapping me.

MENELAUS: What Pharaoh? What kidnapping?

HELEN: You look as if... you must be...

MENELAUS: It's all right. Stand still.

HELEN: You can't get me now. I'm here.

MENELAUS: Who are you? When I look at you, I –

HELEN: And you, who are you?

MENELAUS: So alike... identical...

HELEN: Oh gods! Is it? Can it be... ?

MENELAUS: Are you Greek, Egyptian?

HELEN: Greek. Tell me your name. Tell me.

MENELAUS: Lady, you look like Helen. Identical.

HELEN: And you, like Menelaus.

MENELAUS: I am Menelaus.
            The wanderer, the sufferer.

HELEN: At last. Hold me. Husband.

MENELAUS: What are you doing? Who are you?

HELEN: Helen. Your wife. After all these years.

MENELAUS: Gods, help me. What's happening?

HELEN: It's real. It's true. I'm Helen.

MENELAUS: Two Helens. One man, two wives.

HELEN: What d'you mean?

MENELAUS: In the cave. The other one. From Troy.

HELEN: I'm your wife. No others.

MENELAUS: I don't believe my eyes.

HELEN: I look like someone else?

MENELAUS: How can I know?

HELEN: Trust me, trust what you see.

MENELAUS: How can I?

HELEN: Believe it.

MENELAUS: The other one, in the cave. A dream?

HELEN: A shadow. I'm here.
                  I never went to Troy.

MENELAUS: A shadow that lived and breathed?

HELEN: God moulded it. Thin air: your wife.

MENELAUS: What god? I don't believe it.

HELEN: Hera. For Paris, to keep him from me.

MENELAUS: But how could you be there
                  In Troy, and here?

HELEN: What was there in Troy,

They called it Helen, but I was here.

MENELAUS: It's ridiculous. I'm going.

HELEN: You prefer a shadow?

MENELAUS: I'm sorry. You are like her...

HELEN: I'm dead.
My husband came back, and goes.

MENELAUS: I trust what happened. I was there.
I daren't trust you.

HELEN: Oee eyoh. Nothing left.
My loved ones, my Greece, all gone.

Enter Sailor.

SAILOR: Sir, Menelaus.
I've been looking everywhere.
They sent me, the survivors,
Sent me to find you.

MENELAUS: What's wrong? Enemies, attacking?

SAILOR: You won't believe it.

MENELAUS: Tell me calmly.

SAILOR: All you suffered before, was nothing.

MENELAUS: Tell me.

SAILOR: She's gone. Your wife, sir: vanished.
Into thin air, the sky.
We were in the cave. She said,
'Trojans, Greeks, you died for me,

Troy's rivers ran red for me. Hera did it,
Made me to make you die.
Paris stole me,
You thought I was his - I wasn't.
Now it's over. I'm cloud, I'm air,
I've done what I was made for,
I go home to my father, Sky.
Poor Helen!
She was innocent, innocent -
And the things they say she did!'

He sees Helen.

Oh. Helen. You were here all the time.
Thanks. I was telling him you'd gone,
Grown wings and gone.
We'd enough of your tricks in Troy,
We don't need this.

MENELAUS: What you told me: it's true. All true.
After all these years. Darling.

Music.

HELEN: Husband. After all these years.
Joy's born. Happiness, reborn.
You're here. He's here,
Friends, here, in my arms,
My love, my light.

MENELAUS: After all these years. Hold me.
What can we say?
There's so much to say.

HELEN: My hair's shivering.
Tears. Husband,
Darling, here in my arms.

MENELAUS: What else do we need?
               You're here again, you're mine,
               My Helen, you came to me,
               Torches blazed, women sang,
               You came to me. God snatched you,
               Tore away all happiness –
               And now you're here again.
               All happiness is ours.

CHORUS: Happiness, happiness.
               God bless you both.

HELEN: Look, friends, look:
               My husband.
               No more tears,
               No more waiting,
               After all these years,
               He's here.

MENELAUS: Hold me.
               Ten thousand days
               Wandering, wandering –
               Then this! God gives us this.
               Out of pain, God gives us joy,
               Gives happiness.

HELEN: Hold me. Lean your head.
               Here, on my breasts. Oh joy.

MENELAUS: I thought you'd left me.
               I thought you'd gone to Troy.
               How could it happen?

HELEN: E! E! Bitter memories,
               E! E! The pain of it.

MENELAUS: God's pain. God's gift. Tell me.

HELEN: I spit it away. I can't.

MENELAUS: It's over. Please.

HELEN: It didn't happen.
            Troy-rape, stranger-rape,
            Oars thudding, hearts,
            Didn't happen.

MENELAUS: God stole you.

HELEN: God's son, God's messenger,
            Snatched me here, to Egypt.

MENELAUS: It's incredible, a fairy tale.

HELEN: I cried in it, cried in it.
            Hera hurt us.

MENELAUS: Hera? We offended her?

HELEN: Hurt on that mountainside,
            Those pools, goddesses bathing,
            Gleaming, Paris judged them, judged...

MENELAUS: And then Hera -

HELEN: She was jealous. Hurt him.

MENELAUS: How?

HELEN: Stole me from him. Aphrodite's gift.

MENELAUS: Unbearable.

HELEN: Snatched me here, to Egypt.

MENELAUS: Gave him a shadow. Ah.

HELEN: But then at home, Leda at home,
              Hurt Leda -

MENELAUS: What?

HELEN: My mother, dead. She believed
              What they said of me. She was ashamed.
              She hanged herself.

MENELAUS: Oh moee.
              But our daughter. Our little one. Alive?

HELEN: Darling, who wants her?
              Who'll marry her, give children?
              Tears are all she has.

MENELAUS: Paris killed us all.
              Killed all our house,
              Killed himself,
              Killed thousands, thousands.

HELEN: God did it. God snatched me
              From home, from you, for nothing.
              Not lust, it wasn't lust. God did it.

                     Music ends.

CHORUS: What's past is past.
              If you're happy now, it's over.

SAILOR: Sir, Menelaus. If I could... if you'd...

MENELAUS: Speak, old man.

SAILOR: The one who killed us all in Troy:
              Not her?
MENELAUS: God cheated us. We fought for a shadow.

SAILOR: Died for a shadow?

MENELAUS: God's will.

SAILOR: This lady is her ladyship?
                 Truly her ladyship?

MENELAUS: Believe me.

SAILOR: *(to Helen)*
                 God's hand, child.
                 Who understands the gods?
                 They do what they like.
                 We're pebbles in a game to them,
                 They move us where they like.
                 We're happy, we're destroyed -
                 No choice, it's up to them.
                 Fill your hands with fortune,
                 Clutch it close - it's water.
                 How you've suffered,
                 You and his lordship.
                 Reputation, battle - for nothing.
                 And now things are well again,
                 Luck's in his hands again.
                 You never shamed
                 His old Majesty, your father,
                 Never shamed the princes your brothers,
                 Never did what they said you did.

                 When I think of your wedding day!
                 All those years ago. I was a torch-bearer,
                 I ran beside your chariot, the two of you,
                 You and his Majesty.
                 Slaves live for their owners,
                 Feel joy for their owners' joy,
                 Pain for their pain.

I'm nothing, a slave,
But in my heart I'm free,
I feel what a free man feels,
I'm not a slave inside.

MENELAUS: Old man, you've played your part.
In the battleline, in the hiss of spears,
You've played your part.
Now share our joy.
Go to the others, my other friends,
Tell them it's all right, it's well, all's well.
They're to stay where they are:
Things to do, her ladyship,
We have to steal her away from here,
We'll need their help.
We must watch and wait,
Work together to end this.
Tell them.

SAILOR: Yes, Majesty. Prophets, ha!
What do prophets know? Lies,
They burn bits of animals on fires,
They listen to birds, they make up lies,
And we believe them!
He could have told us then,
Calchas, told us in Aulis:
'It's nothing.
It isn't Helen, it's a shadow.
If you go to Troy,
Set siege to Troy,
You'll die for nothing, a shadow.'
He could have said that, he didn't. Why?
God shut his mouth? Forget him, then!
Forget all prophets! Sacrifice to God,
Ask God directly,
Ignore what prophets say.
They're in it for the money,

It's conjuring.
Believe your own eyes, own ears:
That's what I say.

Exit.

CHORUS: I think he's right.
Make the gods your friends,
Ignore priests and prophets,
You've all you need.

HELEN: Well, happiness is here. But Troy,
Darling, when you escaped from Troy,
What happened? Was it dreadful?
Tell me.

MENELAUS: You want me to tell you.
That business in Evia,
When Nauplius built fires
On the shore to wreck us?
Crete, Africa,
That sea-monster Perseus killed?
Later, I'll tell you later. We've time.
Not now, now I'm tired.

HELEN: I should have realised.
Just one thing:
How long has it been,
All these long years?

MENELAUS: Ten years in Troy,
Then seven wandering.

HELEN: Feoo feoo.
So many. To suffer
So much, so long,
And then come here to die.

MENELAUS: Die? What d'you mean? Tell me.

HELEN: Go. Don't wait here. Go.
              Unless you go, he'll kill you.

MENELAUS: What have I done?

HELEN: If you're here, he can't marry me.

MENELAUS: How, marry you? My wife!

HELEN: He does what he wants.

MENELAUS: Who is he?

HELEN: Pharaoh.

MENELAUS: Now I understand.
              At the gate: I understand.
HELEN: What d'you mean? What gate?

MENELAUS·   This gate. I knocked. She told me, 'Go'.

HELEN: You... begged here? What will I do?

MENELAUS: It wasn't begging.

HELEN: She told you about...
              Pharaoh, this marriage?

MENELAUS: What he wants, she told me,
              Not what you want.

HELEN: I'm yours, only yours.

MENELAUS: You mean you - ? Darling.

HELEN: I'm here, in the dust, here, this pyramid.
MENELAUS: I don't understand.

HELEN: Sanctuary. No marriage. Sanctuary.

MENELAUS: They do that in Egypt?

HELEN: It's like a temple. God's here, protects.

MENELAUS: A ship. If there's a ship,
        I'll take you home.

HELEN: There's nothing. If you stay, you die.

MENELAUS: How can I bear it?

HELEN: Go. It's all right. Leave me.

MENELAUS: I toppled Troy for you.

HELEN: If you stay for me, you die for me.

MENELAUS: I'm not afraid. I toppled Troy.

HELEN: You'll fight a duel with him, kill him?

MENELAUS: He's not immortal.

HELEN: Force won't help you.

MENELAUS: What then?
        Sit here on my hands, and wait?

HELEN: Make a plan.

MENELAUS: I'll fight before I die.

HELEN: There is one way.

MENELAUS: Money? Force? Persuasion?

HELEN: If he never knows you came.

MENELAUS: I'm not about to tell him.

HELEN: They know, inside.

MENELAUS: The slaves?

HELEN: His sister, Theonoe, Her Reverence.

MENELAUS: She'll tell him?

HELEN: She's a prophetess. Knows everything.

MENELAUS: I'm dead.

HELEN: We could ask her -

MENELAUS: Don't tell me she's your plan?

HELEN: She doesn't have to tell him.

MENELAUS: Even if she doesn't, we've still to escape.

HELEN: Unless she helps us, we're dead.

MENELAUS: A woman. You ask her.

HELEN: On my knees...

MENELAUS: And if she says no?

HELEN: You die;
              They come to me for marriage; tears.

MENELAUS: I don't understand.

HELEN: I swore, by the gods -

MENELAUS: You'd -

HELEN: Die with you. Beside you. Forever.

MENELAUS: Say that again.

HELEN: On the day you die, I die.

MENELAUS: And I, on the day you die.

HELEN: But how do we do it? Where do we do it?

MENELAUS: Here, by this pyramid.
I kill you, I stab myself.
But first, I fight for you. Fight hard.
If he comes for you, demands you...
I fought at Troy, saw Achilles die,
Watched Ajax die, saw heroes die -
Shall I let all Greece say this of me:
'He let them snatch his wife, and lived?'
Gods watch. If a man dies proud
They give him light resting,
But cowards they fling out
On flint, on stone.

CHORUS: Gods, hear us.
The royal house cursed,
Generation after generation:
Make all well now.

HELEN: Oee eyoh. It's happening.
She's coming, Menelaus,
Her Reverence,
They're opening the gates.

Run. Hide. She knows everything,
She'll know where you are. You're dead.
You were saved in Troy,
God brought you here, you're dead.

Enter Theonoe, attended.

THEONOE: Lead the way. Lights! Bring fire
From the sacred hearth, purify the air
I breathe, the path I walk on. I'll pray
To the gods; then in,
Restore the sacred flame.

Helen, all my prophecies were true.
Your husband, Menelaus, look:
Shipwrecked. Your shadow: gone.
And you, sir: to reach this place
After such weary years,
And still not know
If you get home to Sparta safely, or if this
Is where you end. Gods argue the case
Even now, in heaven at Zeus' throne.
Hera, your enemy before,
And now your friend,
Wants you home with Helen,
To show the world
That what Aphrodite did,
What she did to Paris,
That wedding she contrived, was lies.
Aphrodite wants you dead,
Wants what she did kept secret,
Paying bribes to win that contest.
It's up to me, they've left it to me.
If I tell my brother you're here,
You're dead, Aphrodite wins.
If I hide it, Hera wins, you live,
If I disobey my brother.
He gave strict orders:

If you landed in Egypt,
He was to hear of it.

(to the Attendants)
One of you, find his Majesty. Tell him
The man he asked about, is here.

HELEN: Your Reverence, I'm kneeling, begging.
For myself, for my husband.
All these years I wept for him,
And now I've found him
I must weep again.
Don't tell your brother
He's here, he's in my arms.
Help us. I'm on my knees.
Lust, your Reverence,
Unholiness:
If you do as your brother asks
You're part of it. God turns his face
From violence: we should own
What we own by honesty, not force.
We have the sky, it's common,
We've Mother Earth, room for all,
We don't need to snatch
What others own.
Hermes brought me here,
Saved me from piracy,
Gave me to his Majesty
Your father to protect,
Keep safe for Menelaus.
Bitter safety, but essential.
And now he's come,
My husband's come, he wants me back.
If he's murdered,
How can he take me home?
Give the living to the dead - is that
What his Majesty your father said?

What's ours, what's rightfully ours,
That's what each of us should have.
He wants it, your father wants it,
God wants it. Listen to him,
Your father, not your brother
Who spurns the gods. Your Reverence,
You see all, know all: shame on you
If you reject justice, your father's justice,
And side with your brother's wickedness.
Know past and future,
And not know right from wrong!
Help me, my sea of troubles,
Rescue me, such a little gift,
It's nothing. The whole world knows me,
Spits on me: she betrayed her husband,
Troy's golden houses gleamed,
And off she went.
If I get home to Greece, to Sparta,
They'll see it's not true, it was the gods,
Gods did it, Gods ruined them,
I'm innocent, I was faithful,
They'll see, they'll understand.
My daughter: no one wants her now,
But then I'll lead her wedding-songs.
I'll be queen again, her Majesty:
Here, I'm nothing.
If he'd died in Troy,
I'd have wept for him -
Am I to lose him here
Before my eyes, and weep?
Please, your Reverence.
Be like your father,
Be loved as he was loved.
What greater honour
Could any child,
Any son or daughter, ask?

CHORUS: You fill our eyes with tears.
                 But Menelaus. Menelaus.
                 What does he say?
                 It's life or death for him.

MENELAUS: Tears, kneeling, not for me. I can't:
                 Not after Troy.
                 Even heroes weep, they say.
                 I deny it. I won't.
                 If your mind's made up,
                 If a stranger comes, a husband,
                 Wants what's rightfully his,
                 His own wedded wife,
                 And you grant it, so be it, we're saved.
                 If you don't, if our agony continues,
                 You're a wicked woman.
                 I've arguments. Fair arguments.
                 I'll put them to your father,
                 Here in his tomb.
                 Perhaps they'll move you too.

                 My lord, bedded here in stone, hear me.
                 Give her back to me. Zeus sent her,
                 Menelaus' wife,
                 Asked you to keep her safe.
                 Your daughter, lord:
                 Speak from the grave, tell her.
                 Your honour, lord, if she agrees,
                 Your shame if she refuses.
                 You're in her hands.

                 Hades, lord below, speak for me.
                 For this woman's sake
                 I heaped your halls with dead.
                 Fair dealing, I paid your price.
                 Now give them life again
                 And send them back,
                 Or help this woman outdo her father,

So wise, so fair, and let my Helen go.

If you snatch her away, Egyptian,
I'll tell you what'll happen. (*She* didn't.)
It's an oath, your Reverence:
We've sworn an oath.
First choice: I'll fight your brother,
One of us will lose,
And that's an end of it.
But if he won't, if he's scared of me,
Tries to trick us
Or starve us out of sanctuary,
It's decided:
I kill her first, then turn my sword
And stab myself. Our blood drips down,
Poisons these stones. Our corpses rot,
Pollute your father's grave.
Your shame, your fault.
Your brother doesn't marry her,
No one marries her. She's mine,
Mine for ever - if not on Earth, in Hell.

That's all. Time for deeds, not tears.
Women weep, men act. So, kill me,
If that's what you want.
Be forever shamed.
Or listen, do what's right,
Give me back my wife.

CHORUS: Your Reverence, it's in your hands.
           No one will argue. Please, decide.

THEONOE: Fair dealing. I must, I shall.
           For my own sake, for my father.
           Pander to my brother? Stain myself?
           My reputation? No. Her Reverence,
           My father's daughter: I stand for justice.
           Hera wants to help you;

I vote as she does.
Aphrodite, love-goddess,
Has no power here -
Lifelong chastity, sacred vows,
Her Reverence.
You talk of shame:
My father's, this place -
And mine, if I refuse.
He'd have given her back,
And so do I. She's yours.
We're human:
What we do stands for us or against us
In the afterlife.
Our bodies die, but our souls live on,
Our essence, that never dies.

All right. I'll say nothing. What you ask,
My brother and his...
Foolishness, nothing.
It's for his own good, he'll thank me later.
But it's up to you now. Find a way out:
You, yourselves, I won't help you.
Nothing. I'll stay impartial.
Pray to the gods:
Aphrodite to bring Helen safely home,
Hera to bless you both,
Keep you safe, still safe.

Father, in your name I do this:
Your honour, your reputation,
Are safe with me.

Exit with Attendants.

CHORUS: Do right: it's the only way.
             If you're dishonest, you'll fail, always.

HELEN: Menelaus, we can trust her.
              But it's up to us now. Up to you.
              How do we get away?

MENELAUS: Right. You know the palace.
              You've lived here for years.

HELEN: What shall I do?

MENELAUS: Ask for a chariot. Persuade them.

HELEN: Then what? It's desert.

MENELAUS: You're right. Take me inside, then,
              Hide me. I'll kill him inside.

HELEN: Don't be silly. If she thought
              You were going to murder him,
              She'd warn him.

MENELAUS: What else can we do? We need a ship.
              The one we had is sunk.

HELEN: Got it! Sorry, a woman's plan -
              But if we put it about you're dead...

MENELAUS: God help me. Still, if it works... All right.

HELEN: We'll do what women do:
              We'll weep, we'll wail, chop our hair.

MENELAUS: What good will that do?
              We're trying to get away.

HELEN: Exactly. I'll say you drowned
              In that shipwreck.
              Ask him to let me bury you *in absentia*.

MENELAUS: *In absentia*. We still haven't got a ship.

HELEN: Yes we have. I'll ask for one. I'll say
               You died at sea, must be buried at sea.

MENELAUS: And if he says 'No. On land.'?

HELEN: I'll tell him it's what we do in Greece.

MENELAUS: So you sail out to sea...
               I hide in the ship...

HELEN: And your crew...
               The ones who didn't drown...

MENELAUS: I'll be the captain. There'll be fighting.

HELEN: You can see to that. If we just set sail... !

MENELAUS: It'll work. With God's good help...
               All right, I'm dead -
               Who brought you the news?

HELEN: You did. You sailed with Menelaus,
               Shipwreck, you were the sole survivor.

MENELAUS: I'm certainly dressed for it.
               Fishing-nets, not finery.

HELEN: You see, we use everything.
               Even that shipwreck works out for us.

MENELAUS: Shall I come in with you,
               Or wait out here, in sanctuary?

HELEN: Stay here. If he tries anything,
               Use the god,
               And if not the god, your sword.

I'll go in, chop my hair,
Change these white clothes
For black, scratch my cheeks for grief.
It's risky. Only two ways out of it:
They find out what's going on, I'm dead,
Or it works and we both get home.
Queen of Heaven, Hera,
Look down on us. Save us.
We lift our arms to you,
Lady, star-throned. Aphrodite, lady,
You bartered my happiness
To win a prize, help me.
You smeared me once,
Left my body but stole my name -
Make that enough. If you insist I die,
Let me die at home in Sparta. Lady,
Why this thirst for harm? Spells, tricks,
Potions, rip homes apart - for what?
Be satisfied. We love you, lady,
In all but this we love you.
O grant my prayer.

Exit. Music.

CHORUS: Leaf-canopy, dark trees,   [*strophe*]
                You nest there, sing there,
                Songs all of tears,
                Sweet nightingale,
                Sing for us,
                Feathers throb for us,
                Weep for us,
                Sing pain, Helen's pain,
                Their pain, the wives of Troy.
                See where he skipped,
                Skipped across grey sea,
                Paris, bridegroom, blood-groom,
                Fetching her, fetching her,
                Death for Troy.

Spears, stones,   [*antistrophe*]
Greeks died for you,
Wives wept for you, wept,
Chopped hair for you,
Their husbands who died for you,
Died in the battle-roar,
Died in Troy,
Died there in grey sea,
Dark rocks, grey sea,
Died on that ship,
Menelaus' ship,
Cargoing her home,
No wife, no living wife,
A shadow.

Who understands the gods?   [*strophe*]
Whose mind leaps the gulf
Between mortals, gods,
Hears their secrets,
Comes back to tell of it?
Helen, Helen for example:
Zeus' daughter, beating wings,
Mother's lap, seed planted -
And they call her liar, cheat, whore.
Who can understand, explain?

Who knows where honour lies?   [*anti*strophe]
Spear-points, battle-lines -
Will you find it there,
End mortal pain?
Blood drowns out argument.
Helen, Helen for example:
They could have talked for her,
They chose to fight for her.
They're dead, in Hell. Troy's gone,
And still all she has is pain.

During this, Helen has come out, dressed in
mourning, and is hiding with Menelaus. As the
music ends, enter Theoclymenus, with Guards.

THEOCLYMENUS: Pharaoh, father, I salute you:
As always, going or coming,
Salute you, there where you lie.

Take the nets inside, the dogs.
There's trouble. I blame myself.
Death, I decreed: all criminals, death.
And now there's a Greek, they say,
Slipped past the guards. A spy,
Or perhaps it's Helen he's come for.
Catch him, he's dead.

Ea.
It's happened. She's gone.
The sanctuary. She's gone.
Open up! Now! Horses, men,
War-chariots! I want her,
She's mine, she mustn't get away.

Wait! She's here. Two of them, here.
You, why black? Black clothes,
Chopped hair, why? Torn cheeks.
You've dreamt something. Bad news
From home. What is it? Speak.

HELEN: I'm dead, Majesty. All's gone.

THEOCLYMENUS: What are you talking about?

HELEN: Menelaus... oee moee... he's dead.

THEOCLYMENUS: I'm sorry. Glad, sorry, both.
Who told you? Her Reverence?

HELEN: This man. He was with him.

THEOCLYMENUS: He told you?

HELEN: Yes.

THEOCLYMENUS: That man, there?

HELEN: In sanctuary. Exactly.

THEOCLYMENUS: Those rags! What he's suffered!

HELEN: What my husband's suffered.

THEOCLYMENUS: How did he get here?

HELEN: He's Greek. Sailed on Menelaus' ship.

THEOCLYMENUS: How does he say your husband died?

HELEN: Drowned, lord. It's dreadful.

THEOCLYMENUS: Where drowned? Somewhere local?

HELEN: Some part of the sea. Somewhere.

THEOCLYMENUS: So how did he not drown?

HELEN: Lords die, slaves live: it happens.

THEOCLYMENUS: So he didn't drown.
                Where did he leave the ship?

HELEN: Where I wish he'd died,
                And my husband lived.

THEOCLYMENUS: Menelaus drowned,
                And he reached land. How?

HELEN: Fishermen rescued him, he says.

THEOCLYMENUS: And that... other thing,
                    Troy's doom - what of that?

HELEN: My shadow? Vanished.

THEOCLYMENUS: O Priam, Troy, all gone - for this!

HELEN: I, too, destroyed.

THEOCLYMENUS: Menelaus' corpse - have they buried it?

HELEN: Not yet. As you see...

THEOCLYMENUS: That's why you chopped your hair.
                    Lovely hair.

HELEN: For love of him. Oh, I see him, still.

THEOCLYMENUS: She's raving. Out of her mind with grief.

HELEN: Suppose your own sister, lord,
                    Her Reverence -

THEOCLYMENUS: She's alive. Come away from there.

HELEN: I can't. My husband: I must be faithful.

THEOCLYMENUS: Still playing games! He's dead.

HELEN: You're right. It's time. I'll marry you.

THEOCLYMENUS: At last!

HELEN: No more arguing.
THEOCLYMENUS: What's past is past.

HELEN: Forgive me.

THEOCLYMENUS: What's to forgive?

HELEN: And grant me -

THEOCLYMENUS: Anything. What?

HELEN: Let me bury my husband.

THEOCLYMENUS: His body's lost.
                  Would you bury a shadow?

HELEN: Greeks. When people die at sea,
                  We do that.

THEOCLYMENUS: You've a custom for everything.

HELEN: We bury empty robes.

THEOCLYMENUS: Do it then.
                  Dig a grave, anywhere you like.

HELEN: Oh, not when someone drowns.

THEOCLYMENUS: What d'you mean? Hairsplitting, now.

HELEN: We take all the offerings to sea.

THEOCLYMENUS: Whatever you say.
                  What exactly do you need?

HELEN: Ask this man here. I never had to -

THEOCLYMENUS: You. I gather, good news for me.

MENELAUS: Not for us, not for him who died.

THEOCLYMENUS: Well. Lost at sea. What kind of burial?

MENELAUS: Whatever we can afford.

THEOCLYMENUS: Forget the money. Tell me the details.

MENELAUS: Blood-sacrifice, for the gods below.

THEOCLYMENUS: Any animal in particular?

MENELAUS: You choose, lord. Anything.

THEOCLYMENUS: A horse? A bull?

MENELAUS: So long as it's unblemished.

THEOCLYMENUS: I think we can rise to that.

MENELAUS: Clothes, even though there's no body.

THEOCLYMENUS: Nothing else?

MENELAUS: Weapons, armour.

THEOCLYMENUS: He'll have what his rank deserves.

MENELAUS: Other things: fruit, flowers, the usual.

THEOCLYMENUS: What d'you do with them?
                Throw them in the sea?

MENELAUS: From a ship. A fast ship, rowers...

THEOCLYMENUS: How far out to sea is this?

MENELAUS: Where no breakers can be seen on shore.

THEOCLYMENUS: Another Greek custom. Why?

MENELAUS: To prevent waves washing them in again.

THEOCLYMENUS: A war-galley, then. It's yours.

MENELAUS: Menelaus thanks you.

THEOCLYMENUS: Does she need to go?
                          Can't you do it alone?

MENELAUS: It has to be
                          The mother, the wife, the children.

THEOCLYMENUS: Her, then.

MENELAUS: Her duty to the dead.

THEOCLYMENUS: She can go. A dutiful wife...
                          You go inside,
                          Choose what you need. Do this well,
                          You'll be well rewarded.
                          You won't leave Egypt empty-handed.
                          Decent clothes, not rags like these,
                          Food, safe conduct,
                          A great improvement.

                          Helen, be comforted. He's gone,
                          You won't bring him back with tears.

MENELAUS: He's right, young woman. Duty:
                          Obey the husband you have, no other.
                          Accept your fate.
                          When I come to Greece
                          I'll see the whole world
                          Knows what happened,

Forgets what it thought of you before.
Just be loyal to your husband,
A loyal wife.

HELEN: Yes, sir.
He'll have no complaint, my husband.
You'll be there, you'll know.
Now come inside.
Hot bath, clean clothes, all you need -
I'll see to everything. For his sake,
My dearest of men, my Menelaus:
If I'm good to you,
You'll do all you can for him.

Exeunt all but Chorus. Music.

CHORUS: See her then,   [*strophe*]
Rushing, rushing,
Mountain mother, Demeter,
Hillsides, rapids, roaring seas -
Where is she, my daughter,
Stolen, where stolen?
Drums, rattles, shrieking,
Wild animals, harness them,
Harness them, she was dancing,
Her maidens, whirling, dancing.
Hunt her, find her, Demeter, mother,
Artemis, Athene, hunt her - No!
Sky-shine, Zeus says no, it's over.

Stopped in her tracks,   [*antistrophe*]
No searching,
Mother robbed, Demeter,
High crags, snow-eyries, ice-peaks,
Weeping, tears echoing,
Snowfields, icefields, echoing.
Blight mortals! No harvest,
Green fields, standing crops,

All gone, all gone. Flocks, dead,
Cities dead, gods' altars dead.
Streams dry, no rivers, bright water,
Tears for her daughter, flint heart,
Flint tears for daughter gone.

Zeus spoke.   [*strophe*]
'Our sacrifices, dead.
Her rage, her mother's rage.
Go now, go to her,
Graces, Muses, sing to her,
Dance to her, soothe her.'
Dancing then, drums, cymbals,
Smiling flute, Aphrodite smiled,
Sweet music.

Helen!   [*antistrophe*]
You wronged her, angered her,
Demeter, all-mother,
Scorned her, ignored her -
Fawnskins, ivy-dancing,
Hair whirling, whirling -
All-mother, you scorned her,
Made light of her, your beauty,
Cursed yourself.

Music ends. Enter Helen.

HELEN: Friends, all went well, inside.
                 Her Reverence didn't tell -
                 Her brother asked, she knew,
                 She didn't tell. 'He's dead,' she said,
                 'Menelaus, buried, sees no more sun.'
                 She helped us, helped us.

                 Menelaus seized his luck.
                 Chose weapons to drown in the sea:

A shield, a spear, well-fitted.
'To honour the dead,' he told them -
But he was practising, practising,
Finding the weight of them, ready,
If they come after us, if all Egypt comes,
He'll stop them.
I found new clothes for him,
He stripped his rags, he bathed,
Fresh water, I drew it,
Water from the well.

His Majesty's coming.
He thinks I'm his,
I'm waiting to marry him.
Don't speak, keep our secret safe –
And one day soon,
When we're safe from here,
We'll save you too.

       Enter Theoclymenus, Menelaus and Attendants
       with the objects for the funeral ceremony.

THEOCLYMENUS: You're under his orders.
Do exactly what he says.
Helen, stay here.
I'm sorry, I want you here.
Go or stay,
You've done what you had to do
For Menelaus.
I don't want you drowning,
Remembering him,
Throwing yourself overboard -
You loved him.

HELEN: Husband - how strange it sounds! -
How can I help remembering?
I loved him, I'd have died for him: once,

Not now. He doesn't need my death.
Let me go, pay these last respects,
That's all I ask. I pray the gods
To grant you... all I pray for you,
And him, this fellow who's helping us.
Grant what I ask, for me, for Menelaus -
You'll see what a wife I'll be to you,
What a wife you've earned.
Do it, lord,
For luck's sake do it, give the orders,
Tell them to launch the ship.
For my sake, lord.

THEOCLYMENUS: *(to an Attendant)*
You. A galley. Fully crewed. See to it.

HELEN: The stranger still in charge?

THEOCLYMENUS: My men will obey him.

HELEN: Tell them again. Make doubly sure.

THEOCLYMENUS: *(to Attendant)*
Do what he says. To the letter. Do it.

HELEN: I ask for nothing more.

THEOCLYMENUS: Don't cry too much. Your lovely eyes...

HELEN: I won't. I'll do all you ask.

THEOCLYMENUS: He doesn't need tears. He's dead.

HELEN: He needs no tears.

THEOCLYMENUS: I'm here. You've got me. I'm yours.

HELEN: If fate and the gods agree.

THEOCLYMENUS: It's up to you.

HELEN: Where my heart should be: I know.

THEOCLYMENUS: I'll come with you. Help you -

HELEN: No, lord.
              Your slaves, leave it to your slaves.

THEOCLYMENUS: Greek customs! I'll leave them to Greeks.
              He didn't die here,
              Our palace is clean of him.

              You. Go in. Wedding-preparations.
              Celebrations, rejoicing, order them:
              Helen, your prince:
              All Egypt must sing for us.

              (to Menelaus)
              Take this stuff, friend. Give it to the sea,
              The waves' embrace, for Menelaus -
              Then hurry back,
              Bring Helen back, my wife.
              I want you here,
              Our wedding, honoured guest -
              And after that, go home,
              Or stay with honour here.

                    Exit.

MENELAUS: Zeus, all-wise you are, all-father,
              See what we do, protect us,
              We're dragging against disaster,
              Stretch out your hand and save us:
              Fingertips, lord, we'll triumph.
              Pain we've had, our share of it,
              Now end it. God hurts, God heals -

Zeus, hear me, help me,
Out of long suffering grant luck at last.

Exeunt all but Chorus. Music.

CHORUS: War-galley, mother of oars,   [*strophe*]
Lead the dancing,
Fast, deep water,
Dolphins dancing,
Oars bending, bending,
Pulling our lady home.

There by the riverside   [*antistrophe*]
Horses running,
Running, dances,
Night-dances, lights,
Your daughter waiting,
Marriage-torches waiting.

Cranes make us, cranes,   [*strophe*]
Gathering, flocking,
Harsh voices calling,
Over grey sea calling,
Clouds racing,
Troy down, Menelaus home.

Castor, Pollux, come,   [*antistrophe*]
Soaring, swooping,
Wind-bringing, sea-skimming,
Grey sea skimming,
Racing, racing,
Lead Helen your sister home.

*Music ends. Enter Theoclymenus and Servant,
separately.*

SERVANT: Disaster, lord,

In the house, disaster.

THEOCLYMENUS: What's happened?

SERVANT: All your wooing, wasted.
She's escaped. She's gone.

THEOCLYMENUS: This is Egypt.
On wings, you mean? Running?

SERVANT: Menelaus took her. It was him.
That survivor.
He announced his own death.

THEOCLYMENUS: Outrageous. But how did it happen?
They had a ship?

SERVANT: You gave them one, lord.
Your ship, your sailors. Gone.

THEOCLYMENUS: I still don't see... There was one of him,
There were dozens of sailors.
How could he...?

SERVANT: She left the palace,
Zeus' daughter, left you.
A procession. We took her to the shore.
Slowly she walked,
Moaning, lamenting
As if he was dead,
The husband beside her.
We went to the docks. A galley, fast,
Exactly as ordered. Fifty oars,
Sails, helmsman... We took our places.
We were making ready still,
When a group of Greeks appeared
Out of nowhere. Menelaus' men,

They'd been waiting. Rags. Sea-stained.
Bedraggled. Soldiers, shipwrecked,
Down on their luck.
He said, Menelaus said,
Put it on for our benefit, 'Poor souls!
Have you, too, been shipwrecked?
Greeks: Come on board, help us,
Menelaus' funeral,
This is his wife, poor lady, he's drowned,
We're holding a memorial.'
Oh, they caught on. Tears.
Picked up the stuff, climbed on board.
We didn't like it.
Too many of them for comfort.
But we'd orders, your orders,
To do what he said. We bit our lips.

Soon everything was loaded.
Except the bull.
It bent its head, bellowed.
Rolled its eyes.
The gangplank was steep and slippery.
Sharp horns: we didn't dare go near.
Then he said, 'Greeks, you toppled Troy,
Show Greekness now. It's just a bull.
Get it on board. If you have to, lift it.
Menelaus' sacrifice, the dead one.
Here, you: a knife: prod it.'
They swarmed on it, lifted it,
Dumped it on deck.
He stroked its flanks, its muzzle,
Soothed it. We finished loading.
Last of all,
Helen climbed on board,
White feet on the ladder,
Took her place next to Menelaus,
The husband we'd been told was dead.
The rest of them ranged themselves,

This side, that side.
They were hiding knives.

'Cast off!' the order came. We rowed.
Stirred sea to foam. Well out to sea,
Not out of sight of land, but far enough.
'Stop rowing! Sir Greek,
Will this place do,
Or should we row still further?'
'This'll do.'
He lifted his sword, cut the bull's throat,
Prayed - they weren't funeral prayers.
'Poseidon, sea-nymphs,
This blood for you.
Carry me home, safe home.'
Blood spurted,
Fountained on the sea: a good omen.
One of us said, 'This is a trick.
Turn back. Give the order. Now.'
Menelaus said - still red with blood -
'Now, Greeks, now! Kill the enemy,
Smash them, drown them.'
'Protect yourselves!' your bosun shouted.

Spars, oars, benches,
We did what we could.
But they had knives.
Deck swam with blood.
If you slipped, you died.
She was standing there,
Shouting them on.
'Do what you did in Troy.
Barbarians: kill them, kill them.'
Menelaus led them,
Full armour, sword in hand,
What else could we do?
Dived overboard,
Swam for our lives.

His men took the oars,
Turned the ship for Greece.
Sails up. Fair wind.

That's all. They're gone.
I'd let myself down by the anchor-rope.
Fishermen found me, rescued me,
Or else I'd have drowned. Now I'm here.
Bad news. As the proverb says,
A trust mislaid is a trust betrayed.

CHORUS: Menelaus, here!
And no one noticed, lord:
No one noticed, not you, not us.

          Music.

THEOCLYMENUS: Tricked! Women! Eyoh talass!
Marriage gone, ship gone, all gone.
She'll die for this.
Inside, she'll die for this.
Sister no sister, she knew he was here,
Menelaus here, said nothing.
She'll die for this.

          *He runs to the gate. The Servant struggles with
          him.*

SERVANT: No, lord. What are you doing?

THEOCLYM: Punishing. Killing. Out of the way.

SERVANT: Sir, wait. You can't.

THEOCLYMENUS: Slave, let go.

SERVANT: You mustn't.

THEOCLYMENUS: I said, let go.

SERVANT: Sir, no.

THEOCLYMENUS: I'll kill her.

SERVANT: Her Reverence.

THEOCLYMENUS: Her wickedness.

SERVANT: She had to.

THEOCLYMENUS: Had to steal my wife?

SERVANT: Not your wife, his wife.

THEOCLYMENUS: She was mine, mine.

SERVANT: He married her first.

THEOCLYMENUS: Fate gave her to me.

SERVANT: And took her away again.

THEOCLYMENUS: Swap arguments?

SERVANT: I tell the truth.

THEOCLYMENUS: Who's Pharaoh here?

SERVANT: Rule justly, justly.

THEOCLYMENUS: You'll die for this.

SERVANT: If I die, I die. But you won't kill her,
                Your sister, Her Reverence,
                While I'm alive to stop you.

I'm hers, her slave. I'll die for her.

Melée. Enter Castor and Pollux. Music ends.

CASTOR:

Stop it. King of Egypt, stop it.
Castor orders it, Pollux, sons of Zeus.
Be calm. Our sister's gone, Helen,
The one you're shouting about –
That marriage: gone. Forbidden. Fate.
Don't blame your sister, Her Reverence:
She did what was right.
God ordered, she obeyed.
The gods sent Helen here, for a time,
Safe-keeping, while they borrowed
Her name to topple Troy.
Now it's done,
She can go back home,
To her family, her husband.
We could have rescued her long ago,
Our sister – we're gods,
Zeus has made us gods –
But we were overruled by Fate,
Subject to stronger powers,
A grand design.

Helen, far out to sea now, hear us.
Sail home with your husband.
Fair winds, for home.
We're with you,
We're riding the waves
To bring you home.
Live happily.
As soon as your time on Earth is done
You'll join us, here in the sky: you'll be
A goddess, worshipped. Your shrine
Where Hermes first gathered you,
Plucked you from Sparta, from Paris,
To bring you safe to Egypt. As for you,

Menelaus, your wanderings are over.
Your life will end now peacefully,
You'll live in the Islands of the Blessed.
Helen, Menelaus:
Not exactly nobodies,
Not to suffer forever.
God loves aristocrats.

THEOCLYMENUS: Sons of Zeus,
I hear you, hear and obey.
I lay down my arms.
My sister's safe.
And Helen's safe -
To go back home
As the gods decree.
You're lucky - who else in all the world
Had such a sister?
So trusting, honest, long-suffering -
None like her, no other woman like her,
Not now, not in the past, not ever.

CHORUS: God springs surprises, always.
Expect the unexpected.
What mortals dream, the gods frustrate;
For the impossible, they find a way
That's what happened here, today.

Exeunt.

BACKGROUND MYTHS

Not all the gods were happy with Zeus' rule. Poseidon and Apollo conspired against him, and he punished them by making them serve for one year as slaves to a mortal. The mortal was King Laomedon, and the gods built him a city, Troy. Its walls were invulnerable wherever the gods built them; in the one place where Laomedon's men worked on them, they were breakable - and this was the place later pulled down to let the Trojans pull in the Wooden Horse.

In the generation after Laomedon, his son Priam and Priam's queen Hecuba ignored a warning from the gods that the child in Hecuba's womb was a firebrand which would destroy Troy. The child was Paris, and his parents let him live, merely changing his name to Alexander and sending him from the city to grow up on the royal estates on Mount Ida. Here three goddesses asked him to choose the most beautiful, and each offered him a prize if she were chosen. Hera offered military glory; Athene offered dominion; Aphrodite offered Helen of Sparta, seduction incarnate, the most beautiful woman in the world. Paris chose Aphrodite, and soon afterwards sailed to Sparta and stole Helen from her husband Menelaus.

Menelaus and his brother Agamemnon (who was married to Helen's twin sister Clytemnestra) gathered a huge Greek fleet to win Helen back. Each state sent men and ships, and the leading heroes of Greece, men such as Achilles, Diomedes and Odysseus, all went to war. The fighting lasted for ten years, but at last, thanks to Odysseus' strategy of the Wooden Horse, the city fell.
The victorious Greeks sacked Troy, gathered the booty and assembled the women for distribution. Their leaders cast lots for the highest-born women. Queen Hecuba was allotted to Odysseus; Andromache (wife of Hector, the Trojan prince killed by Achilles) was allotted to Achilles' son Neoptolemus; Cassandra, Hecuba's daughter (a prophetess who had long foretold the fall of Troy) was allotted to Agamemnon - and foresaw her own death, and his, at the hands of Agamemnon's wife Clytemnestra as soon as they reached Mycenae.

While the captives were waiting for distribution, three things happened to unhinge Hecuba's mind. The Greeks took her baby grandson Astyanax and killed him in case he grew up to rebuild Troy. They butchered her youngest daughter Polyxena as a blood-sacrifice over Achilles' tomb. And the body of her son Polydorus, whom she had sent for safekeeping to an ally she thought was trustworthy, Polymestor, was washed up on the beach. Until now, she had suffered with dignity; now she took revenge on Polymestor, blinding him and killing his own two sons; then, before Odysseus could take her and load her on to his ship, she turned into a dog howling and baying for vengeance, ran into the sea (or, some say, jumped from the tip of the mast of Odysseus' ship) and drowned.

The Greeks loaded their booty and set sail. But the gods who had supported the Trojans, especially Poseidon, gave them difficult and bitter homecomings. Menelaus planned to take Helen back to Sparta and kill her there. But, in some accounts, her brothers, the Heavenly Twins Castor and Pollux, took her into heaven to become a will-o'-the-wisp, a seductive light guiding sailors lost at sea. In other accounts, she sailed with Menelaus, and during the voyage seduced him into forgiving her. In yet another, the 'Helen' he loaded into his ship - the 'Helen' who went to Troy - was not a woman at all, but a cloud moulded by Hera into an exact replica of Helen. The real Helen (Menelaus' true and loyal wife, not the flirtatious and death-bringing monster all Greece thought her) was taken by the gods to Egypt, where she sat out the war, waiting for her husband to discover where she was and rescue her.

WHO'S WHO

(NB For further details, see BACKGROUND MYTHS. Stressed sylla-bles in capital letters. Asterisked names have entries of their own.)

ACHILLES (a-KILL-ees, Greek a-chil-EVS, 'man of grief'). Most powerful of the Greek heroes at Troy; killed *Hector.

AEGYPTUS (e-GIP-tuss, 'he-goat'). Legendary founder of Egyptian race, brother and rival of *Danaus.

AEROPE (e-ROH-pi, 'sky face'). Wife of *Atreus and mother of *Agamemnon and *Menelaus.

AGAMEMNON (ag-a-MEM-non, 'total resolution'). Ruler of Mycenae in Argos, warlord of Greece.

AJAX (AY-jax, Greek AI-ass, 'great of the Earth'). Greek hero at Troy, brother of *Telamon.

ALCMENA (alk-MEE-na, 'might of the moon'). Mother of *Heracles.

ANDROMACHE (and-ROM-a-kee, 'battle of men'). Wife of *Hector, mother of *Astyanax.

APHRODITE (a-fro-DIE-tee, 'foam-born'). Goddess of sexual attraction.

APOLLO (' destroyer'). God of disease, healing, music and prophe-cy: the Sun's light, deified. His oracle was thought infallible.

ARCADIA (ar-KAY-dee-a). Particularly beautiful region of central Greece.

ARES (AH-rees, 'invincible'). God of war.

ARGOS (AR-goss). Agamemnon's kingdom, centred on the citadel
of Mycenae. It was here that Queen Clytemnestra (Helen's
sister) ruled while he was away at the War; she later killed
him in revenge for the sacrifice of their daughter Iphigenia.

ARTEMIS (AR-te-miss). *Apollo's twin, virgin goddess of the
Moon, of hunting, and of women.

ASTYANAX (ass-TY-an-ax, 'city-lord'). Infant son of *Hector and
*Andromache.

ATHENE (ath-EE-ni). Goddess of wisdom and war, patron of
Athens.

ATREUS (AT-tr-yooss). Father of Agamemnon and Menelaus.

CALCHAS (KAL-kass, 'bronze'). Greek priest and prophet during
the Trojan War.

CALLISTO (ka-LISS-toh, 'most beautiful'). Mountain-nymph,
raped by *Zeus and then turned into a bear (the Great Bear
in the heavens).

CAPHEREUS (ka-FER-yooss). Mountain and sea-girt cliffs on the
island of Evia, where *Nauplius lit beacon-fires to attract
passing sailors on to the rocks.

CASSANDRA (kas-ANN-dra, 'entangler of men'). Daughter of
*Priam and *Hecuba. She promised to sleep with *Apollo if
he gave her the gift of unerring prophecy, then refused - so
that he added to the gift the twist that although she was
always correct, no one would ever believe a word she said.

CASTOR. Son of *Zeus and *Leda, twin of *Pollux, brother of
*Clytemnestra and *Helen. The twins were taken into heav-
en and made stars, responsible for guiding ships lost at sea.

CHARYBDIS (ka-RIB-diss, 'gullet'). Sea monster in the form of a whirlpool, who engulfed ships passing overhead.

CIRCE (SER-see, 'falcon'). Sun's daughter, sorceress.

CLYTEMNESTRA (kly-tem-NESS-tra, Greek klu-ti-MESS-tri, 'famous wooing'). Twin sister of *Helen, and wife of *Agamemnon.

DANAUS (DAN-a-uss). Legendary founder of Greek ('Danaan') race, brother and rival of *Aegyptus.

DEMETER (dee-MEE-ter, 'barley-mother'). Goddess of harvest. After her daughter *Persephone was stolen by *Hades to become queen of the Underworld, Demeter refused to allow any growth or harvest on Earth, until *Zeus intervened, allowing Persephone half her time in the Underworld, half in the world above.

DIOMEDES (di-o-MEE-dees, 'cunning of Zeus'). Greek hero, famous for his exploits with *Odysseus at Troy.

EPEUS (e-PAY-uss, 'attacker'). Greek craftsman who built the Wooden Horse.

EUROTAS (yoo-ROH-tass). Wide, beautiful river of Sparta.

GANYMEDE (GAN-i-meed, Greek Gan-u-MEE-dees, 'rejoicing in virility'). Handsome Trojan prince, taken by *Zeus to be cupbearer of the gods.

HADES (HAY-dees, Greek a-EETH-ees, 'invisible'). *Zeus' brother, ruler of the Underworld.

HECATE (hek-AH-tee, 'one hundred'). Goddess of midnight and black magic.

HECTOR. Eldest son of *Priam and *Hecuba, senior hero of Troy.

HECUBA (HEK-yoo-ba, Greek e-KA-vee, 'moving far off'). Wife of
      *Priam, queen of Troy and mother of over fifty children.
      After her change into a bitch and her death (see Background
      Myths), the Greeks set up a monument called Cynossema
      ('bitch-lighthouse'), on the peninsula now called Gallipoli.

HELEN (Greek e-LEE-ni, 'moonwoman'). Twin of *Clytemnestra,
      wife of *Menelaus, (alleged or actual) lover of Paris.

HELENUS (HEL-e-nuss, Greek e-LEE-noss, 'moonman'). Prophet
      son of *Priam and *Hecuba.

HEPHAESTUS (hef-I-tuss, 'dayshine'). Blacksmith-god, husband
      of *Aphrodite.

HERA (HEE-ra, Greek EE-ree, 'protector'). Consort of *Zeus and
      queen of Heaven.

HERACLES (HER-a-klees, 'glory of Hera'). Greek hero, son of
      *Zeus and *Alcmena. Cheated by King *Laomedon of Troy,
      he sacked the city and killed the king, leaving *Priam (then a
      baby) on the throne.

HERMES ('pillar'). Messenger-god.

HYMEN (HIGH-men). God of the marriage-union.

LAOMEDON (la-O-me-don, 'ruler'). Trojan king for whom
      *Apollo and *Poseidon built the walls of Troy. Laomedon
      later quarrelled with *Heracles, who killed him.

LEDA (LEE-da, 'lady'). Queen of Sparta, wife of *Tyndareus.
      *Zeus took the form of a swan and raped her, and she laid
      two eggs, one hatching into *Helen and *Clytemnestra, the
      other into *Castor and Pollux.

LETO (LEE-toh). After (unsuccessfully) taking the form of a quail to escape being raped by *Zeus, she gave birth to *Apollo and *Artemis on the island of Delos.

MENELAUS (men-i-LAY-uss, 'leader of the people'). *Agamemnon's brother; *Helen's husband.

NAUPLIUS (NO(r)-pli-uss [silent 'r'], Greek nav-PLEE-oss, 'navigator'). King of Evia, who hated the Greeks and lit fires along his rocky coastline to attract their ships on to the rocks as they sailed home from Troy.

NEOPTOLEMUS (ne-op-TOL-e-muss, 'new war'). Fierce Greek hero at Troy, son of *Achilles.

ODYSSEUS (o-DISS-yooss, Greek o-thee-SEVS, 'angry'). Greek hero famous for his deviousness; among other things, he devised the trick of the Wooden Horse which toppled Troy.

OENOMAUS (ee-no-MA-uss, 'fighting drunk'). King of Pisa in Greece, murdered by *Pelops.

PARIS (PA-riss, 'wallet' or 'scrotum'). Son of *Priam and *Hecuba who judged the beauty contest of three goddesses, stole *Helen from *Menelaus and began the Trojan War.

PELOPS (PEL-ops, 'clayface'). King of Argos. To win a wife, he challenged *Oenomaus to a chariot-race, and substituted a wax axle-pin for the real one. Oenomaus died- the beginning of the curse on Pelops' descendants, the house of Argos.

PENEUS (pe-NAY-uss). River.

PERGAMUM (PER-ga-mum). Old citadel of Troy, before the god-built walls were made.

PERSEPHONE (per-SE-fo-nee, Greek fer-se-FASS-a, 'teller of destruction'). Queen of the Underworld.

PHOCIS (FOH-kiss). Small village not far from Delphi, centre of Apollo's oracle.

PHTHIA (f-THEE-a). Inaccessible part of northern Greece.

POLLUX (Greek Polydeukes, 'much sweet wine'). Son of *Zeus, brother of *Castor, *Clytemnestra and *Helen.

POLYDORUS (pol-i-DOH-russ, 'many gifts'). Youngest son of *Priam and *Hecuba, sent for safe-keeping to Thrace before the Trojan War, but murdered by King *Polymestor.

POLYMESTOR (pol-i-MESS-tohr, 'much-mindful'). King of Thrace who killed *Polydorus and suffered for it.

POLYPHEMUS (plo-i-FEE-muss). One-eyed giant on Sicily who attacked Odysseus and his crew as the returned from Troy.

POLYXENA (pol-IX-e-na, 'much-friended'). Youngest daughter of *Priam and *Hecuba, sacrificed by the Greeks on *Achilles' grave.

POSEIDON (po-SAY-don, 'drink-giver'). Brother of *Zeus, ruler of salt and fresh water, god of earthquakes.

PRIAM (PRY-am, 'bought ruler'). King of Troy, husband of *Hecuba.

PSAMMATHE (psa-MAH-thee, 'sandy'). Sea-nymph, mother of *Theoclymenus and *Theonoe.

SCAMANDER (ska-MAN-der, 'crooked'). River of Troy.

SCYLLA (SILL-a, 'bitch'). Sea monster with a girdle of fanged dogs' heads on snake-necks, who snatched and ate sailors.

SIMOIS (SIM-o-iss). River and marsh near Troy.

SIRENS. Sea-monsters whose singing lured sailors to disaster.

TALTHYBIUS (tal-THIB-i-uss). Senior non-commissioned officer
    of the Greek navy, admired for his diplomatic powers and
    used as a mouthpiece of the High Command.

TELAMON (TEL-a-mon, 'darer'). King of Salamis, one of the
    Greek heroes at Troy, father of *Ajax and *Teucer.

TEMPE (TEM-pi). Beautiful river-valley, out of which rose Mount
    Olympus, home of the gods.

TEUCER (CHEW-ser, 'builder'). Son of *Telamon, brother of
    *Ajax. Banished from Salamis, he wandered the world to
    found a new city.

THEOCLYMENUS (the-o-KLIM-e-nuss, 'renowned by God').
    Pharaoh of Egypt.

THEONOE (the-o-NOH-e, 'knows about the gods'). Egyptian
    prophetess, sister of *Theoclymenus.

THESEUS (THEES-yooss, Greek thee-SEVS, 'establisher'). King
    of Athens.

TITHONUS (ti-THOH-nuss). Trojan prince loved by the goddess
    Dawn, who forgot that he was mortal, and grieved as he aged
    and withered before her eyes.

TYNDAREUS (tin-DA-re-uss, 'pestle'). King of Sparta, husband of
    *Leda, father of two of *Castor, *Clytemnestra, *Helen and
    Pollux. (The other two were *Zeus' children. As they were all
    conceived on the same occasion, it was impossible to say
    which children were whose.)

ZEUS (one syllable, but please not 'Zoos'; add the 'y' of 'your', ie
    'Zyooss'; Greek Zefs, 'shining sky'). Supreme deity, ruler of
    the visible world.